# RUNNING YOUR OWN BUSINESS MADE EASY

# LAWPACK

# About the author

Roy Hedges is a freelance writer, entrepreneur and consultant. His practical business guides draw on extensive hands-on experience of starting up, buying and selling businesses himself, ranging from retail grocery outlets to garages and property. His career as an entrepreneur peaked when a firm of bankers' agents that he started grew into a finance company with seven branches, offering trade and consumer finance facilities, before becoming a bank. From this subsidiary, insurance, property and leasing companies emerged. Later, he was to become one of the founding directors of London Trust Securities and Equilease Commercial Finance Ltd. More recently, Roy has been a director of a leading management consultancy and a board member of the leasing subsidiary of a major trade financier and invoice discounter.

Besides addressing manufacturing and trade association gatherings and small business forums on various business topics, he lectures in business studies at Havering College of Further Education and has broadcast on BBC Radio Essex.

Running Your Own Business Made Easy
by Roy Hedges

First edition 1999
Second edition 2002
© 2002 Law Pack Publishing Limited

## LAWPACK

76-89 Alscot Road  London SE1 3AW
www.lawpack.co.uk
All rights reserved.

ISBN 1 904053 26 2

# Table of contents

# Introduction to Running Your Own Business

## *You have a dream*

Sometimes the desire to become self-employed or start a business just isn't enough. Certainly it will give you many new and exciting adventures, but it will also mean you can no longer rely on others to make decisions for you, or lead the way. True, you will take charge of your own destiny, but being in charge also means facing up to the responsibilities that come with being your own boss. Not anyone can run a successful business. It needs commitment, self-reliance and determination.

It can be very lonely making decisions. Any mistake, and the buck stops with you. The way you live and work will alter, which at the beginning might not be for the better. The initial twelve to eighteen months of any business are crucial. You can expect to work longer hours for less pay and experience feelings of insecurity and isolation. Nevertheless, if you have the right characteristics, a good idea, the capability to plan ahead, and the persistence to overcome any setbacks, then having your own business can be extremely rewarding.

There has never been a better time to start up a business than today, even though the business environment is constantly changing and throwing up fresh challenges. Today's entrepreneurs are better informed, have more help available to them and with the lowest interest for decades, money should no longer be a problem.

This second edition is bursting with all the information you need, from locating the best Internet sites to new sources of finance and more. As you expand you'll be creating jobs, so a new section relating to employment contracts has been introduced. The section on buying supplies has been expanded and there are several new tips on how to promote your business on a shoestring.

The key to success in business is you. Knowing your personal strengths and vulnerabilities will allow you to combat any lack of experience you may have. Learning vital new skills will build self-confidence before you venture into the alien environment of self-employment. Setting up your own business is not just about setting up a stall, hoping that customers will flock to buy your wares. There is much to learn and do before that day dawns. Fortunately, you will not be alone; you'll have help every step of the way.

# Is running a business for you?

1

# Chapter 1

## Is running
## a business for you?

Running your own business or becoming self-employed can bring rewards and stimulating challenges that working for somebody else never will – if you have the right frame of mind. But knowing where to start can be so confusing. Therefore, the best place to start is with yourself. That makes sense, doesn't it? For example, do you constantly say to yourself?

- I want my own business but I'm not sure if I've got what it takes.

- I know I could run this firm better than my boss.

- I'm in a dead end job. How can I take control of my life?

- Can I get a business idea that will work?

If you answered yes to any of these, then perhaps you should be taking the first steps towards forming your own business. But first, take the time to discover if you have what it takes to make your business work.

Going into business with the wrong temperament can be very costly and disappointing. Doing your own thing isn't for everyone. There are no guarantees for success. However, if you have only some of the qualities or skills required, all is not lost. You can change, learn new skills and prosper. Running a business is about putting yourself into other people's shoes and predicting their requirements. Knowledge such as this can be acquired. The following list highlights a few of the most essential characteristics required:

- **Self-starter.** You must be able to identify business opportunities as they arise and confidently act upon them without assistance from others.

- **Determination.** It will take all the determination you can marshal to get your business off the ground.

- **Self-discipline.** Working on your own, sometimes outside normal working hours, will require a high level of self-sufficiency.

- **Accountability.** Blaming others if things go wrong is not possible. The responsibility of being in charge of your business must be enjoyed, not feared.

- **Innovation.** You will need to come up with better methods of operating and new ideas to give your customers the service they deserve on a continual basis.

- **Enthusiasm.** Being enthusiastic about your plans and products gets others involved. It also keeps customers and bank managers on your side.

**DEFINITION**

Management means providing leadership for your employees, answering their many questions and making decisions that could affect their lives.

There are lots of people running flourishing businesses who have neither qualifications nor training. They might lack some of the above traits, but they would not have succeeded without commitment, will power, a competitive streak and the ability to work extremely long hours. The chances of succeeding diminish quickly unless you can find these things inside yourself. Use the following Self-Assessment Questionnaire to discover to what degree you possess these needed traits. Be honest with yourself when answering the questions. Nothing is gained by being untruthful. The only person you hurt is yourself.

Read each question or statement carefully. Reflect on how strongly you either agree or disagree with it. Show how you identify with each remark by scoring from 1–10 at the end of each statement. For example, 1 will indicate you disagree with the question. On the other hand 10 will signify that you strongly agree, i.e., it sums up your character precisely.

In respect of the question: Do I perform well under pressure? If you concur that you do perform well when under pressure, enter 10. If you feel your work deteriorates under pressure, enter 1. If you believe working under pressure makes you feel uncomfortable, but your work doesn't suffer, enter 4. etc, etc.

## Self-assessment questionnaire

Your score
out of 10

1. Do I perform well under pressure? _____

2. Do I stay calm and not get stressed? _____

3. I resent influences over which I have no control, affecting my life. _____

4. Can I work with, and lead a team? _____

5. I don't like starting something I am unable to complete. _____

6. Does making decisions come easily? _____

7. Are the decisions I make usually the right ones? _____

8. Am I positive, and do I enjoy taking risks? _____

9. Am I happier when I do not have to rely on other people? _____

10. Do I work well using my own initiative? _____

11. Do I bounce back from setbacks and work at a problem until it's solved? _____

12. Is the thought of learning new skills and the responsibility of being my own boss exciting me? _____

13. Do I have the ability to change my mind when it's obvious an earlier decision was wrong?  _____

14. Does explaining things to others come easy, and am I ever misunderstood?  _____

15. Would my partner or I object to business interfering with our private lives?  _____

16. Am I a good listener, and can I take advice from others?  _____

17. I prefer to stand alone, than to be one of a crowd.  _____

18. Meeting and dealing with different people is something I enjoy.  _____

19. Having my success recognised by others is important to me.  _____

20. I am at present in good health, and rarely get sick.  _____

**TOTAL:**  _____

When you have answered all of the questions and statements, total your score. Look on the next page to see how you shape up to becoming an entrepreneur. If in doubt give your completed assessment questionnaire to a friend or relation you trust. Ask them for a fair appraisal of your abilities. Don't be afraid of criticism. Learning to accept your faults is another trait you'll need in your armoury. Learning to conquer your failings is the bedrock of successful businesses.

## *Assessment results*

Look for the group into which your score falls. In addition, also reconsider any scores which were either extremely high or low; assess how accurate you have been.

180-200    If your score lies in this band, stress and pressure spur you on. You are dedicated and prepared to work hard to achieve your goals. The risk and insecurity of running your own business will motivate rather than worry you. You have every chance of success with the right business idea and sound planning.

140-179    Certain aspects of running your own business may give you problems. The severity of these will depend on your determination to overcome adversity. Concentrate on improving those areas where you did not have a high score. However, you seem to have the right frame of mind to deal with the day to day pressures of running a business. Your business should flourish and you'll probably enjoy the rewards more than those with a higher score.

100-139    If your scores varied wildly, such as a lot of 1,2,8, and 9's, you must try and improve the lower scores. Otherwise those regions could be the source of severe problems if you are unable to change them. If this score was reached with reasonably consistent scoring, you should have no cause for concern, but must ensure you have a good business plan and be prepared to make use of the various training schemes.

60-90    If your responses were born out of uncertainty, contact your local enterprise agency for details of training courses. While you may have the ability to run your own business there are strong indications that you will not enjoy it. Not enjoying your business could cause you to give up under the slightest pressure. Think long and hard about whether you really want to run a business. If you still think going into business is for you, make use of the help and training that are readily available.

Under 60    Running you own business will be a strain – one you may not wish to endure for long. Running a business requires confidence, self-reliance and the competence to handle stress and pressure. Without these traits it would be unwise to set up your own business. You should find out about training courses in your local area to develop the skills you lack.

The above assessment results are only a general guide which assumes the assessment of yourself was frank and truthful. It is not an appraisal of your technical and commercial proficiency, but of your personal attributes which could affect your business. It's basic, and is intended to give only a broad idea of your aptitude. Contact your local Training and Enterprise Council (TEC) today for details of courses in your area, since even with the right personality and attitude, some skills instruction may be required.

## *Personal objectives*

There are usually many reasons for becoming self-employed; they will have a strong bearing on the direction and growth of your business. Your aims can have a direct effect on the success or failure of the business, therefore, they should be considered very carefully.

One of the most common causes for someone to want to run their own business is the dissatisfaction they feel when working for someone else. Another might be the belief that you can offer a better product or service than is currently available. Whatever it is, it's important for you to establish your objectives and to know what you want out of your business. You will find it easier to construct your business plan when you are aware of what you expect to gain from the enterprise. Plotting your course carefully will allow you to monitor the progress you and your business are making towards your goals. You'll need the ability to juggle many tasks and the self-assurance to ask questions.

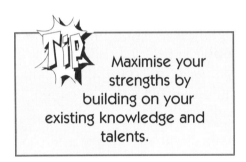

Maximise your strengths by building on your existing knowledge and talents.

Other thoughts that lead people into running their own business include:

- the wish to spend more time with the family

- the desire to create a new business, help it grow and mature

- the need to pay off a mortgage in five years

- the hope of gaining independence

- the wish to attain a certain level of income (e.g. £100,000 p.a.) within a specified time scale

Did you notice that the motivation behind many of these is the acquisition of money? Being motivated by money alone could mean you spend all your time chasing profits, to the exclusion of everything else. Whilst every business needs to be profitable, remember that profits are generated from satisfied customers. Your customers will pay for what they want – not what you wish to provide them. They will not tolerate inferior goods or services. So if you're going into business just for the money, never lose sight of the fact that your customers must always come first.

Some people want to go into business for themselves but are undecided on the type of business they want to conduct. They may have more than one business idea, or they might wish to consider other options before reaching a decision. Perhaps they are simply seeking a new idea in order to expand an existing business. Whatever business idea you decide upon, it must be something you enjoy doing, or are comfortable with.

Business ideas have many origins but they should never be taken in isolation. Many ideas can compliment each other to form a final business idea. Potential sources are:

- **Hobbies and interests.** There have been lots of successful businesses born out of a hobby or pastime. You do need to check that your hobby can be turned into a viable business proposition. Remember that while it is easy to get carried away with something you really take pleasure from, not everyone will share your enthusiasm.

- **Personal experience & training** are good sources of inspiration. Experience gained working for somebody else can lead to profitable ideas, as well as professional or vocational training. Do check out opportunities on your doorstep, such as the industry you are currently working in. This will give you added advantages because when you start up your business customers will already know you, thereby creating an instant rapport. This will help to get your new enterprise off to a flying start.

- **Copying or spin off products.** This does not mean plagiarising someone's patent, design or ownership rights. If you should come across a product not available in your area, it may be a good idea to introduce it locally. You may also come across a product or service that with a few changes could meet an alternative market. However, you must get permission from the creator of the product or service. Be careful not to infringe on any registered designs or patents. Take legal advice. It is far better to run a business you have been trained in than to enter a field that is unknown to you.

- **Existing businesses or franchises.** You may wish to take over an established business or purchase into a franchise operation. This option provides an instant business, but will not necessarily remove the risks. A franchiser will have a direct interest in ensuring your success and will work with you in order to get you established, which could include helping to find suitable premises and training.

- **Inventions**, which you have developed, can give you an edge in business. It is advisable to protect your invention by applying for a patent and registering the design. The address of the patent office can be found on page 120, at the end of Chapter 7.

# *Putting down the right foundations*

Knowing what you want from life and having the correct skills and attitude means that you can start to lay a strong foundation for the business of your dreams. However, when you are self-employed, you will need to juggle different sorts of tasks. While you cannot be expected to possess the knowledge of an accountant or personnel manager, you will probably have to learn new skills to ensure that you have the rudimentary ingredients of any profitable business.

Training is available, both for those who are already in business as well as those who are still in the planning stage. Such training implies spending months in preparation before opening the doors of your business, but without a doubt, the time and effort that you put in will be time well spent.

Some of the skill shortages you may face are:

- **Management.** Whether working alone or with others, you must be able to manage and control your business.

- **Financial.** It is important to know your business has sufficient funding and cash flow for it to operate. Simple bookkeeping knowledge will be sufficient, but don't forget that getting paid on time is crucial!

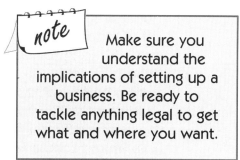

note

Make sure you understand the implications of setting up a business. Be ready to tackle anything legal to get what and where you want.

- **Sales & Marketing.** Learning how to keep your customers supplied with what they require and how to make a profit by doing so.

- **Production & Transportation.** If you manufacture the products you are selling, you must guarantee your goods meet with your customer's requirements and that the goods are delivered as required.

You may not need to have an in-depth knowledge of all these subjects, merely a basic understanding, since it is possible to buy these skills in, as and when the demand arises. Knowing which fundamental skills are needed, and how to keep your business running profitably can be the basic building block of success.

## *Turning dreams into realities*

*note* No two businesses are alike. Whatever type of business you choose it will have its own set of requirements. The hazards facing someone who proposes working from home, without additional staff, will be completely different from a limited company planning to open a chain of computer game retail outlets.

Making sure you have all the information needed before starting to trade is essential. There are a number of business support agencies just waiting to hear from you, so if you are unsure where to start, look in your local 'Yellow Pages' for one of the following:

* Business Links

* Chambers of Commerce

* Training & Enterprise agencies

\*   Adult Education Centres

Never be afraid to ask questions. One of the major causes of business failures is lack of insufficient information. Make certain you are adequately prepared for what lies ahead.

In a nutshell, being in business means keeping an open mind about new ideas and overcoming any skill shortages you may have through training. Above all, it means that you do not take short cuts but prepare yourself thoroughly. Keep a list of your personal objectives to hand at all times. Never lose touch of your original targets. Accept responsibilities cheerfully, and enjoy your business.

# Will your ideas work?

# Chapter 2

## Will your ideas work?

The best product or service in the world is of little value unless there are people who want to buy what you have to offer. It is therefore essential to have a viable marketing plan before you go into business.

Time and effort spent on reliable market research will be rewarded many times over. Such research will not only tell you who your customers are but will also provide you with a

*note* Marketing is about giving your customers what they want, when they want it, and at a price that is worthwhile to you both.

very clear indication of why they will buy your goods or services and not those of your competitors. It will also inform you what your potential customers have in common. For example, if the majority of your customers enjoy sailing, it would pay you to advertise in a yachting magazine, or perhaps to set up a stall at one of the boat shows held around the country. Advertising your products in cycling periodical, however, would be a complete waste of money.

**A good idea alone will not guarantee you success.**

Conducting such research should also provide you with valuable insight into the current state of whichever market you decide upon, and it will answer these two essential questions: Is there a market for my product or service? Can I get an adequate market share to make my enterprise worthwhile?

Good market research should reveal answers to questions like these:

* Where are my potential customers situated?

* How can I sell to them?

* What social, legal, political, and economic factors affect the market?

* What are the strengths and weaknesses of the competition?

* What market share can I achieve?

* What prices should I set, and what terms of trade should I offer?

Once you have obtained this information, you will then need to look further into trends in the market place, potential customers, competitors and test marketing. It should be borne in mind that while these sections are inter-related, they will be dealt with individually here in this book.

Much of the information you require can be gained without leaving your home. Your first port of call should be the media. Television, the Internet and newspapers – both national and local – give very useful trade data. Trade magazines are

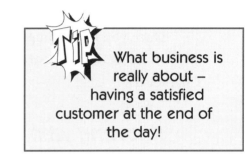

What business is really about – having a satisfied customer at the end of the day!

another specialist reservoir of information. In addition, most banks have a business department which should provide valuable facts and figures on industry trends, and Business Links (The Department of Trade and Industry) will provide you with statistics on both the home and export market. Do not forget your local Chamber of Commerce, trade association, or your local council. Your regional reference library should keep reports created by any of the above bodies. If they don't, they will always point you in the right direction.

When analysing your findings take into account any regional or seasonal trends.

Consider the following when examining your findings:

1. What is the size of the market locally, nationally, or internationally?

2. Is the market expanding, contracting or stagnating?

3. What is the per cent of change?

4. Is the market volatile?

5. Is there any legislation, or technical, economic, or environmental changes taking place at the moment that may affect the marketing of my product or service in the future?

Once you have completed your research write down your findings. They will be needed to construct your business plan, demonstrated for you in Chapter 6.

## Knowing who your customers are

> *note*
>
> Customers will come in all shapes and sizes, but they all have one thing in common, the desire to buy your goods or services.

It will be helpful to construct a customer profile for each product and service you propose to offer. Marketing professionals use the following grades to define social status groups:

| Social grade | Occupational group |
|---|---|
| A | Top management, administrative and professional |
| B | Intermediate managerial |
| C1 | Supervisory, clerical and junior management |
| C2 | Skilled manual workers, pensioners |
| D | Semi-skilled and unskilled manual workers |
| E | Unemployed, casual labourers |

**Classification could also be based on characteristics and common interests shared by your customers.**

Other ways to classify groups of customers are:

- Sex, age, ethnic group, marital or parental status

- Education, skills, culture, religious, or political beliefs

- Profession, occupation, self employed, financial

- Geographically, habits, hobbies, height, and weight

- Industry, no. of employees, turnover exceeding a specific figure

- Special events, marriage, sports, or clubs

- Ownership of, cars, pets, and houses

An average customer profile could be a mixture of classifications. For example, a travel agent specialising in winter sunshine holidays may target people over 60, on the basis of geography – nationally, socially – Grades B and C, and by interest – they might have an interest in walking. A wallpaper manufacturer would target wholesalers and trade outlets instead of individuals. Additionally, the manufacturer might take the financial status or company size (those customers likely to order in excess of £3,000, for instance, in a stated period) into consideration.

Apart from dividing up your customers into quantifiable categories, you will also wish to classify your customers by what they want. Identifying your customers' needs is more likely to bring about the success of your business than anything else. After all, no customers, no profits! So how do you find out what the customer wants? Ask them – both the new and existing customers – what they are looking for and then combine this with the information

Some people only gather information when they are starting up. Failing to keep track of how markets are developing, and what their competitors are up to could be a disastrous. Don't fall into this trap!

gained from your research in market trends. These answers will provide you with a good idea of what people want and how much they are prepared to pay for it.

Customers are really only interested in what your product or service will do for them. They are looking to fulfil a desire. Examples of customers' needs fall into the following general divisions:

- product reliability, after sales service and support

- right product, right quality, flexibility, delivery and competitive price

- honesty, fulfilment/satisfaction, pleasing service and environment

- confidence in your expertise, status, generous terms of trade

Even when you have identified your customers and made sure your product or service meets their needs, your pricing policy may still dramatically affect sales.

## Pricing your goods or services

Pricing is a very delicate matter and as studies have shown, you must get it right the first time. Prices that are too high will cause your customers to go elsewhere. Prices that are too low will make you little or no profit. Undoubtedly, it is a very sensitive area. Most small businesses tend to over-emphasise the importance of price and undercut their competitors. This can lead to bankruptcy or liquidation. Instead, it would be wise to compete on factors such as quality, or service, before taking the drastic step of cutting prices.

Price is not always the overriding factor. A carpenter targeting Grade B house owners was inundated with work by recommendation because of his honesty. The customers needed to leave the carpenter alone in their homes and needed to trust him implicitly. Due to the manner in which he fulfilled their trust, the actual price of his work in these circumstances was not an issue. Honesty, reliability and solid workmanship carried the day.

TIP A well-constructed pricing policy not only ensures you operate your business profitably. It will also help you make the most of your opportunities.

So what do you need to know when it comes to pricing your goods or services? It is important to work out all your costs as accurately as possible. These come in two categories: fixed costs, such as rent, lighting, heating, wages and insurance, and variable costs, which can increase or decrease depending upon the level of business activity. Examples of variable costs include bad debts, raw materials, transport, postage, and packing.

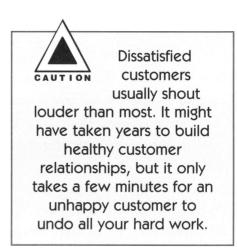

Check other
suppliers for bulk
discounts and other offers
like extended credit.

Watch out for hidden costs, such as wasted stock or materials, depreciation, and the full costs for providing service.

Don't overlook value-added tax (VAT). This is applied to goods and services, and is currently 17.5%, except on household fuel. Your sales must reach a certain threshold before you need to register for VAT. Your local Customs & Excise office will send you the relevant details.

## Promoting and selling your wares (on a shoestring)

Whether you are trying to entice new customers or satisfy existing ones, quality and image count. If the conception you are promoting is appealing, and the product or service you are offering is appreciated, then pulling in and retaining customers should not prove difficult. It's more cost effective to keep existing customers than to have to replace them. Of course, you will have to remind them from time to time of what you do or sell and for what values you stand for. This is what advertising is all about!

CAUTION
Dissatisfied
customers
usually shout
louder than most. It might
have taken years to build
healthy customer
relationships, but it only
takes a few minutes for an
unhappy customer to
undo all your hard work.

Your reputation is a priceless commodity. It takes a long time to acquire and can be lost all too quickly. Recommendations made by satisfied customers cost nothing, but can increase your turnover more quickly and more consistently than any expensive advertising campaign ever will.

Creating a good concept need not cost you the earth. Answering the telephone in a polite, business-like manner costs nothing. Printed stationery items including letterheads, invoices and business cards can be produced relatively cheaply these days. Money is usually tight in small businesses, so you must make every penny count. Take every opportunity to ask customers how they heard of you. If possible, keep a record of their replies – this will tell you what advertising has been effective and what hasn't.

Resources to use for sales promotions might include:

- Business and telephone directories

- Local newspapers and trade magazines

- Direct mail, cold calling

- Internet, some websites are free

- Brochures and leaflets

- Trade fairs and exhibitions

> *note* All some businesses need to get started is a telephone, fax, and access to the Internet to become international traders.

With the advent of reasonably priced PC's, the production of quality brochures or leaflets is no longer the expensive exercise it once was. However, churning out the same old type of material as your competitors will not win you new customers. Most brochures and leaflets I come across tell the same basic story. True, you must let prospective customers know about your business and its products but do it in such a way that makes your sales literature stand out. It must be so interesting that people will want to read it from cover to cover, then tell their friends about it and not simply throw it into the waste bin. In amongst your sales blurb, place snippets of interest. Photographs are always a good idea, and add useful tips or an odd recipe or two. Naturally these additional comments should enhance your goods or services and will differ depending on the type of business you are running. The size and content of this extra material will also vary depending on whether you are producing a leaflet or a brochure, and if you can get a local celebrity involved so much the better.

The type of business you are in will usually dictate the form of your promotions. If your products or service are unique, or if there is some aspect of your business that is newsworthy, you could perhaps ask your trade press or local paper to publish an article about your business – that's called public relations. Local radio stations are often a part of the media overlooked by small businesses when it comes to promoting their firm but they are very interested in hearing about local business.

You might also be able to associate your firm with local charities or other good causes. Public relations is about creating awareness of your business, as opposed to inducing direct sales.

As long as you have new and existing customers, the selling process should never stop. Always be prepared

> **TIP** The best way to increase sales is to convince your regular customers to buy other products or services from you.

and be confident in your product or service. If selling directly to customers yourself, make sure you address the decision-maker. Your time is valuable, so don't waste it. When conducting a sale, you should strive to create a situation where both you and your customer come away from the encounter feeling satisfied with the result.

Here are some pointers to ensure that this happens:

1. **Determine the customer's needs.** Ask questions that will encourage a conversation, not 'Yes' or 'No' responses. Listen carefully to what your customer is saying. Discover which product or service you have most that meets his needs. A good listener will always out sell the glib sales patter of the most talkative salesman.

2. **Emphasise the benefits.** Demonstrate to the customer how what you are selling meets his or her needs. Show how your product or service will bring real benefit.

3. **Close the sale.** Be polite but direct and ask for the business. Never hesitate when it comes to closing a sale and taking an order, you've probably spent much time and effort getting to this stage! Always ask your customer why they bought your product or service, as you may be able to use this information in future sales. By the same token, if your customer did not complete a purchase, try to discover why. It will help you to improve your sales technique or product in the future.

4. **If a customer wants to think it over – agree with them.** State that you are not surprised at their request and ask them what part of your product or services they wish to think about. Use this opportunity to clear any doubts from their minds about what your

product can do for them. Now try and close the sale again.

⚠ **CAUTION** More than any other reason, sales are lost because the salesperson did not actually ask for the order.

5. **Negotiate successfully.** You'll need to be a good negotiator, whatever line of business you are in. Since all successful negotiations require some give and take from both sides, the following advice could be of help to you:

- Work out in advance the price beyond which you will not go, then stick to it.

- If questioned on price, explain confidently and clearly why your price is reasonable. Remember to explain the benefits.

- Never make compromises unless you are getting something in return. For example, I'll reduce the price by 2.5% if you pay cash on delivery, or double your order.

⚠ **CAUTION** When negotiating, bear in mind that what is regarded as unimportant to you could, in fact, be valuable to the other party.

- Give way on inexpensive concessions. I'll be flexible on delivery dates if the price is reduced.

It's this sort of bargaining that builds lasting business relationships.

## *Learning about competitors*

You can locate your competitors from a number of sources. The easiest source is the 'Yellow Pages', but your suppliers might be another, if they're willing to tell you who else they supply. For those of you considering going into retail, simply walking the streets will identify many of your potential competitors. In addition, local business clubs, Chambers of Commerce, trade and professional associations can normally help.

> *note*
> Finding no obvious competitors doesn't mean that you'll have the field to yourself – it may mean there is no market for you idea.

One method of finding out about your competitors is to unobtrusively stand outside their premises, taking notes of deliveries, customers, prices and the general level of activity. This sort of surveillance can also supply you with useful information on suppliers or potential customers that you may not have known about. You should make sample observations of each competitor on different days and times.

Try and sample your competitor's products or services and compare them with your own. If this is not possible, obtain their sales and promotional literature. Try to talk to as many of your competitor's customers as you can. Find out why they buy their goods and services. Remember, anyone offering the same, or similar products and services, is a competitor.

Consider the following points when analysing your competitors:

• What gives you an advantage over your competitors?

• What advantages do your competitors have over you?

- Does your product or service have a unique selling point?

All the information you have collected about your rivals, either individually or as a whole, will be needed when putting your business plan together.

## *Finding your market*

Aided by the information you have accumulated in your market research, you will now be in a position to put together a marketing plan. This will summarise your research and show at a glance how you will market your product or service. Moreover, it will project your expected sales figures. Any prospective investor or lender will expect you to be able to predict future turnover and to clearly demonstrate how this will be achieved.

If you have completed your market research correctly, then your marketing plan should be self-evident. This plan will be in the form of a spreadsheet and will provide a breakdown of:

* units sold and price

* targeted market and method of selling

* value of sales, plus monthly and annual forecasts

* promotion and advertising costs

You can do this for each product or service you offer, or for the business as a whole. You must be confident that you can deliver the figures stated in your marketing plan. Some of the information in your marketing blueprint will also be used later in your profit and cash flow forecasts. Now, you might be saying to yourself, 'If I haven't been in business before, how can I be expected to have sales figures from which I make these forecasts?'

The answer is test marketing. Test marketing can be conducted as a supplement to or instead of other research. A well thought out test marketing plan can provide information on many of the areas mentioned in the market research section. In particular, take note of the success rate of experimental promotions. Find out which ones worked and why they did so, not forgetting to list those that were less effective. This will maximise results and reduce costs. Test marketing is a minimum cost venture to measure a market response. In other words, a 'toes in the water' exercise whose main objective is to make potential customers aware of your product or service and gauge the general level of interest.

Trial marketing is the one 'sure-fire' way to find out if your ideas will work. It is not necessary to actually trade to conduct a test market exercise, and it can be done in a number of ways. Forums that will readily assist you in conducting your research are:

- **Advertising.** Place an advert or a series of differently worded adverts in a suitable media. Advertise the product or service or offer further information to those who respond.

- **Websites.** If you have access to a computer it is easy to set up a simple website. Most website providers offer free pages, with guidelines about how to set up your own web page. Just count how many people visit your site each day and what information they are seeking about your goods or services.

- **Mailshots.** Send details to a sample list of potential customers or clients. If, for example, 4 out of every 100 buy from you, valuable information has been gained. You have started to develop a marketing strategy.

- **Leaflet distribution.** The cheapest and easiest to conduct: sample a target group in your area and you will be able to immediately gauge the response.

> **TIP** Having a thorough understanding of the market in which you trade will keep you one step ahead of the competition at all times.

- **Demonstrations.** Arrange to give demonstrations of your product or service to local groups or clubs. Perhaps a large store will give you space. Trade exhibitions are not only a useful way to test market your products or services, but also will enable you to keep an eye on what your competitors are up to at the same time. The level of interest can be instantly gauged – an added advantage.

Whatever method you use, the end results should be sufficient for you to gauge the potential size of the market and should confirm the feasibility of trading in the market segment tested.

## The nuts and bolts of marketing

Gathering marketing information should be an on-going activity. In business, you must always be aware of your main groups of customers and their interests and needs. In addition, you must know the extent to which your products or services go to meet these needs. Above all, continually assess the best methods of getting your goods or services before the customer.

# Do you have sufficient resources?

3

# Chapter 3

## Do you have sufficient resources?

From this point onwards, you should be considering what resources you currently have and those you'll need in the future. At first you may be able to work alone, maybe from home, but you will need premises and personnel assistance once your business takes off. Working from home may sound like fun, but you must learn to separate your business from your home life at the end of the day. Certainly this arrangement will reduce your start up costs, but there will be drawbacks as well. For example, those with whom you share

**CAUTION** Before you set up business at home, check with your local authority and your household insurance policy for any restrictions against this arrangement. Your business equipment, for example, might not be covered by your existing insurance policy.

your living premises might not appreciate giving up 'their' space and might find it difficult being restricted by the close proximity of your work. Customers who visit unexpectedly could prove a hindrance to a happy family life. Furthermore, you may find it hard to stop working and relax when the day is done.

Working from home can also have financial disadvantages. You may have to pay business rate council tax on your home. If you sell your house, capital gains tax may be levied. There may also be restricted covenants in your mortgage document or tenancy excluding certain activities. An accountant and solicitor will be able to advise you on these matters.

Your financial forecasts will have to take into consideration your future requirements in respect of employing or increasing staff, in addition to ensuring separate business premises are suitable for your expanding business.

*note* Here is a rule of thumb guide for working from home: provided your business doesn't create noise or smells and doesn't cause congestion either of people or vehicles, there should be no major problem. Whatever you do, it is advisable to keep on good terms with your neighbours.

## *Operations*

How you intend to operate will need to be included in your overall business plan. This plan will present information to any interested party about the resources you have or will require to achieve your marketing aim and predicted sales targets. You might, for instance, need to cover seasonal fluctuations by using temporary staff or sub-contractors, and this must be made quite clear.

There are obvious pros and cons to running your business from separate premises. On the positive side, a clear professional image would be gained. Your work will also be more self-contained and less likely to encroach on your private life. One considerable disadvantage is the greater risk of theft or vandalism; with no one on the premises overnight, you will need to budget for security measures.

Many people starting out in business use only their own finance. Others need to borrow until their turnover builds up sufficiently. Borrow too much, and you'll pay too much interest. Borrow too little, and you will be unable to meet your expenses.

If you need to borrow to get started, make sure your calculations are correct. You must also be confident your business will generate enough profits to repay any loans within the agreed terms. Don't forget to communicate this confidence to the lender as well! It is possible to produce an accurate assessment of what you will need as well as your ability to repay any loan. A well-prepared cash flow forecast, explained in the next chapter, will show a comparison of your income and expenditure on a monthly basis over the next few years.

## *Premises and equipment*

Previously, we have taken a general overview of the pros and cons of the location of your business. However, for the purposes of this next section, we have assumed you will operate away from your home environment. Whichever arrangement you decide upon, make sure that your business will have sufficient room to grow.

Business premises can be acquired under different guises, some of which are listed here for your information. However you wish to operate, there will be one method to suit you.

- **Freehold or long leasehold purchase.** Since mortgage costs can be prohibitive, this option might contain hidden dangers. Purchasing, meanwhile, can also be a drawback if you expand rapidly and are unable to move into larger premises.

- **Rental or leasing.** Leasing retail, commercial or industrial property on a fixed term is the usual method for obtaining business premises. All property leases will contain conditions to insure the premises. There may also be restrictions on its use. Make sure you understand the terms before signing.

- **Property licence.** This recent phenomenon is available to new businesses and is often referred to as 'easy in, easy out'. Using business premises on licence enables either party

Occupying a property on licence allows you to move into larger premises quickly as your business grows.

to terminate the agreement at a relatively short notice, such as one to three months. This is beneficial to you if you don't know how long you will require the premises, but the arrangement could prove inconvenient if your landlord inconveniently issues notice, particularly if you want to remain in the premises because it suits you and it's convenient for your customers.

Access for your customers, and sometimes your suppliers, is a very important consideration when deciding upon your location. A retailer will benefit in a location where people frequently pass his door. Commercial premises will need easy access or have adequate car parking facilities. Think of the advantage of being sited next to a railway station!

CAUTION The correct site for your business is vital for your business survival. Spend time thinking about the best position for you before committing yourself.

Industrial premises, on the other hand, may be better sited close to a motorway.

## Stock and suppliers

Stock and materials are two other resources that must be considered when completing your business plan. If these are central to your business operation then you must be sure of getting supplies when you need them and at a price you can afford. You will also need to ensure raw materials will be of a consistent quality and high standard.

It is vital to the survival of your business that you continually review your suppliers and the service they give you. By monitoring the prices they charge, and ensuring the goods you order are delivered on time will in turn keep your business competitive. If costs start to rise unreasonably or the service begins to flag and your orders arrive late, look for a new supplier.

When you do find a reliable supplier, don't simply accept the first price they quote, haggle. Ask for 2.5 per cent or 5 per cent off for prompt payment, perhaps you may get more for guaranteeing regular orders. Negotiating lower prices is an art so to assist you, here are a few handy tips:

- Don't start bargaining until you are sure that you want the goods or services.

- Don't give away the price you are prepared to pay.

- Never give way on a point without getting something in return.

- Keep quiet - the one who is speaking is giving away their position.

- Confirm everything agreed in writing.

Remember, every pound you save is better in your pocket than your supplier's.

 To be sure of a reliable supply of raw materials use more than one supplier.

Another important factor to consider is the cost of materials, so obtain quotations from as many different suppliers as possible. Next, use these quotations to convince one supplier to offer you the best deal, such as reduced prices or extended credit. Your business statement should contain the relevance of particular materials in the following points:

- the importance of materials to your business

- reliability of suppliers – do they deliver on time?

- is the quality of supplier constant?

Having sufficient equipment, including office and/or works machinery, to carry on your business is another aspect to bear in mind. Equipment already owned by you can be brought into the business and charged at a reasonable rate. Anything owned outright will become an asset of the business and will increase its worth. Equipment naturally loses its value as it gets older or becomes obsolete, so it will need to be replaced. This is called depreciation.

Equipment can either be leased or hired, instead of being purchased outright. Its reliability, condition and service life needs to be stressed within the body of your business plan. This is essential if you wish to ensure the profitability of your business.

Plans for transportation and distribution must also be considered before setting up your business. For instance, do you have a sufficient number of vehicles and are these vehicles suitable for achieving your goals? When producing your profit and loss forecasts the costs of running all your motor vehicles must be stated, in addition to the details of their ownership.

> *If you'll need to deliver products to your customers, investigate the cost of outside contractors. It may prove more cost effective to use their services than to purchase your own vehicles.*

With regard to any vehicle used for your trade, it is advisable to keep business and private use separate. The taxman will insist upon the two records being kept separate.

## Key personnel

Before you progress very far with your business plan, clarify what sort of key personnel you must have to get your business off the ground. Are you looking to be the owner of a sole trading company, or do you require partners for a partnership, or directors of a limited company? In addition to these essential roles, there may be others who will be central to your business success, such as employees or associates.

A brief CV or a career profile of every person who will be playing a leading role in your business should be included in your business plan. The basic information you need to present on these people is:

> **note**
>
> Keep your business plan updated in respect of new and existing key personnel, especially in regard to training or new qualifications.

- Names, and qualifications

- Relevant experience, and trade knowledge

- How their skills will contribute to the success of the business

This data should be incorporated into an 'Executive Summary' and form part of your operation strategy. A typical career profile can be seen in the case study and specimen business plan in the appendix, to be found at the rear of this guide.

## Employing people

There will come a time when you will become involved in employing people. Maybe not in the beginning, but as you expand. When you were an employee, you had no cause to worry about recruitment procedures, but now you need to know about the pros and cons of taking on staff.

**note** It is essential for you to insure your staff against accident or illness while on company time.

Employing people will remove some of the mundane tasks from your shoulders and will allow you to manage your business more effectively. However, these employees will bring with them extra responsibilities and obligations. The rules relating to conditions of employment are numerous and complex. Minimum wage and maternity leave are just two examples; other rights concerning employees include:

- health and safety

- unfair dismissal

- redundancy

- discrimination on the ground of sex, race, or marital status

There is also the added burden of ensuring the correct amount of tax and National Insurance contributions are deducted from your staff's wages. Advice about these issues can be obtained from a commercial lawyer, an accountant, the Inland Revenue, the Employment Service, the Department of Social Security, the Equal Opportunities Commission and the Health and Safety Executive.

CAUTION Accidents don't only occur where machinery is involved. You can be sued if an employee trips on a loose paving stone or mat.

One thing you must never overlook when employing staff are contracts of employment. These are mandatory agreements between your firm and it's employees. These contracts should be properly drawn up, and a copy given within two months of someone joining your business. Among other things, the contract will contain basic details such as:

- Employee's name.

- Job title - it is a good idea to attach a job specification to the contract.

- Date employment started.

- Holiday entitlement.

- Details of pay - include details of commission payments and bonus if applicable together with information on how these are earned.

- Period of notice required to end employment.

There are a number of other important factors to be included within this document, disciplinary procedures are just one example.

Employment contracts are now a permanent feature of business life and legal advice should be sought when drawing up your contracts to avoid you being faced with expensive legal claims when an employee is required to leave. Fortunately, legal advice should not cost you the earth because good sources of free and low cost legal assistance are just a mouse click away on the Internet.

There are sites on the Internet aimed at businesses just like yours and these provide online employment contracts and useful information. You will be able to download contracts and tailor them to your own requirements. There is a small charge for downloading and customising employment contracts. Details can be found in the list of useful websites at the back of this book.

## Recruiting, and skill shortages

> **note** Ask yourself if you have the right people, with the right skills, in the right place, at the right time, to deliver your marketing plan.

Changing markets, new technology and an expanding business all mean maintaining and improving the skill levels of your employees on a continuous basis. There are three ways to address this problem: training existing personnel, recruiting additional staff and out-sourcing.

- **Outsourcing or sub-contracting.** This option will ensure you have experienced people completing specific tasks for a pre-set period. Payment is often made only when certain targets have been met. The working arrangement between the parties ceases on completion of the contract. Out-sourcing may remove your liability for payment of National Insurance contributions, sick leave and holidays. However, the rates of pay are likely to exceed those of your directly employed staff. Another potential problem to be aware of – out-sourced contractors will lack familiarity with your firm's operations and standards.

- **Recruiting.** In order to justify taking on extra people on a full or part time basis, you will need to group skill requirements into a job description. A job description (or specification) provides the facts about the job – its basic function and responsibilities, as well a brief explanation as to where the employee slots into the chain of command. The job description should also include the required skills and experience the prospective

Remember, if employing temporary staff directly, you must accord them the same employment rights as full time workers.

employee should possess. A good personnel specification and job description will go a long way towards helping you get the right person for the right job.

- **Identifying skill shortages.** There may be some aspects of your new business that will be strange to you. For example, you may know little about book-keeping, but book-keeping is only an extension of keeping a household budget. Although a little more complex, the principles are the same. So whatever the 'grey area', your local training and enterprise agency will be able to help. Just pick up the 'phone!

The areas in which a new business might experience skill shortages fall into the following categories:

- Financial – including bought and sales ledgers, general book-keeping, VAT, PAYE, balance sheets and budgeting

- Sales and marketing – covering personal selling skills, market research, advertising, customer care and product designing

- Personnel and management – which involves managing time, and people, target setting, industrial relations, training, staff appraisal,

dismissal and grievance procedures

- Operations and communications – which embraces production planning, stock control, computer systems, presentation and report writing

- General skills – incorporating company law, business planning and secretarial

- Technical and professional – embodies all of those skills specific to the type of business you are in, i.e., plumbing, interior design, childcare, engineering and bricklaying

The above list only represents a small proportion of the skills required to run and sustain business growth.

## *Training*

Provision for on-going training should be part of your continuous business strategy. An explicit schedule, either for yourself or for staff, will be a pre-requisite for the skill shortage you have chosen to meet through training. By drawing up such a document you will have a clear mental picture of the total costs and hours involved, as well as the

There are a great many training incentives available to business today, via government-sponsored schemes.

end result of such instruction. This is precisely the sort of information that must be communicated to potential investors. A typical training programme will identify:

* the skills being taught

* names of the trainees

* teaching methods, i.e. own or external staff

* tutor and location

*note*

Personnel development and training builds confidence and motivates your staff. Their improved performance will be reflected in your profits.

Training can range from brief instructions followed by a period of supervision showing a new employee how to operate a particular piece of machinery to much longer term methods, like working towards a National Vocational Qualification (NVQ) or a professional qualification. To demonstrate the importance of training in business, the 'Investors in People' initiative was set up to encourage on-going training. 'Investors in People' is a national award presented to businesses that demonstrate commitment and attain definite standards in training. Firms participating in this initiative are required to develop employees' skills in order to achieve the objectives outlined in their business plan. A sample training plan is to be found in the case study at the rear of this book.

## Getting the most from your resources

Planning ahead and trying to predict what additional equipment or staff you may need as your business grows will help you to get maximum use of your existing resources. The right mix of personnel, premises and fiscal resources is crucial to the success of your business.

# Being in control

# Chapter 4
## Being in control

---

**What you'll find in this chapter:**

- ⮕ Survival income
- ⮕ Cash flow forecasting
- ⮕ Profit & loss forecasting
- ⮕ Understanding book-keeping
- ⮕ Sales ledger management
- ⮕ Summing up your finances
- ⮕ Promoting and selling your wares

---

To determine the success of your business, you will need to put in place some financial targets against which you can measure your performance. This means attempting to predict levels of income and expenditure. After you have commenced trading, review the achievement of your business against these targets. Not only will this review tell you if you are successful, but it will also highlight any problems, rising costs or customers who consistently pay too late, for instance, and will monitor your incoming money. You must keep track of your expenditure, however. It will be difficult to know where you stand if you are lacking any form of fiscal information.

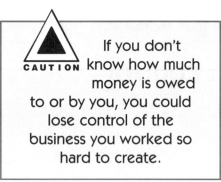

If you don't know how much money is owed to or by you, you could lose control of the business you worked so hard to create.

Forecasting your cash flow requirements over the first twelve months and extending this prognosis into the next two to three years will tell you if you need to raise external finance for your business and if so, how much. It is important to update these forecasts on a regular basis. Initially you can only estimate your requirements, but when trading commences you will be in a position to predict future needs more accurately.

DEFINITION

Working capital is the term used to describe the finance used by businesses for every day trading purposes.

When calculating how much money is needed to set up your business you must take into account the loss of earnings you will suffer. The everyday expenditure of your private life will not go away. Therefore, it is time to look at your personal requirements. After all, one of the main reasons for going into business for yourself was to improve your overall standard of living!

## Survival income

In general you would expect your business to make much more money than is necessary to cover the financial demands of every day private life. Initially, it may take time for your business to generate sufficient turnover to meet the expenditure of the business as well as your income. Therefore, it is essential you do not withdraw excessive amounts to live on. It is useful to know the minimum amount of money you will need to take out of the business to meet all of your personal expenses over a given period. This is called survival income.

When planning survival income always consider a fail-safe element to cover unforeseen occurrences such as a washing machine breaking down.

To determine survival income, you need to establish who makes up your family unit or the number of people who are dependent upon your income. A typical survival budget must also include any income coming into the household, including income from your spouse/partner, investments, or pensions. The resulting total of expenditure over income represents your survival requirements. All items in your forecast should appear net of tax.

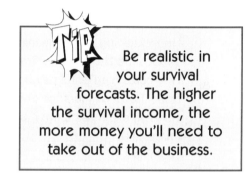

Be realistic in your survival forecasts. The higher the survival income, the more money you'll need to take out of the business.

You also need to determine a time scale over which your survival budget will run. Although this is usually done over a year, some people find it easier to work on a monthly basis. There are four segments to a regular budget and these are usually classified as:

- Domestic expenses, such as rent or mortgage, etc.

- Travel and transport costs

- Personal expenditure like clothing, professional membership fees

- Non-business income

The survival income budget form, shown on the next page, is for you to use.

## SURVIVAL INCOME BUDGET

For . . . . . . . . . . . . . . . . . . . . . . . Period . . . . . . . . . . . . . . . . . . . . £

Mortgage/Rent _____

Council tax/Water rates _____

Fuel (gas/electric etc) _____

Telephone _____

Insurance (property/contents) _____

Housekeeping (food, cleaning etc) _____

TV Licence/Newspapers/Trade Magazines _____

Hire purchase/Rental payments _____

Road Tax and Insurance (motor vehicles) _____

Running expenses (petrol, parking, service) _____

Fares/Taxis _____

Clothing _____

Children's expenses (pocket money etc) _____

Holidays/Christmas/Birthdays _____

Life insurance/Pensions _____

National Insurance _____

Pets (food, vets' bills) _____

Contingencies _____

Total expenditure:

Non-business income (after tax) _____

Family/Partner _____

Investments/Pensions _____

Other (please specify) _____

Total income:

SURVIVAL INCOME REQUIREMENTS:  £
(expenditure less income)

# Cash flow forecasting

There are some very notable differences between forecasting profit and cash flow. The profit estimates show the gain likely to be made in any given time span. It answers the fundamental question: Will the business be viable? The cash flow conjecture shows the planned dates of the movement of money either in or out of the business.

A number of items shown in your cash flow forecast will be identical to those in the profits forecast, although they will be dealt with in a different manner. For example, sales made in June will be invoiced and shown in the June figures. But if they were not paid until two months later, the receipts will be registered in the August cash flow forecasts. This principle also applies to your purchases. For VAT registered businesses, VAT is not a profit and loss item.

> **note** Cash is the lifeblood of every business. Without it, your firm would not be able to operate and flourish.

It will, however, appear in your cash flow forecasts. Receipts that are not profit and loss items include:

- loans

- money invested by the owners

- any capital expenditure

> **note** Having enough cash to pay creditors, wages, and other bills as they fall due is vital to your business survival.

However, the dates these items are due in or out are to be included in the cash flow forecast. Conversely, depreciation is a profit and loss cost to the business but does not appear in the cash flow reports.

Sample *Cash Flow Forecast Guide*

### CASH FLOW FORECAST GUIDE

### For DWR Software

### PERIOD June 2002 to May 2003

| RECEIPTS. | Month: June | | Month: July | |
|---|---|---|---|---|
| | Budget | Actual | Budget | Actual |
| Cash sales | 500 | 2000 | 2000 | |
| Cash from debtors | | | 10000 | 11000 |
| Capital introduced | 5000 | 5000 | | |
| **Total Receipts (a)** | **5000** | **5500** | **1200** | **1300** |
| PAYMENTS. | | | | |
| For goods received | 2100 | 2400 | 9700 | 14800 |
| Salaries/National insurance | 750 | 950 | 1800 | 2100 |
| Rent/Rates | 150 | 150 | | |
| Insurance | 350 | 350 | | |
| Repair & Renewals | | | | |
| Heating/Light/Power | | | 325 | 475 |
| Postage/Printing/Stationery | 1000 | 1200 | | |
| Car/Travelling | | | | 60 |
| Telephone | | | 210 | 290 |
| Professional fees | | | | |
| Capital payments | 3000 | 2500 | 1000 | 1000 |
| Interest charges | 75 | 110 | 150 | 200 |
| VAT payable (refund) | | | | |
| Drawings | | | 1500 | 1250 |
| **Total Payments (b)** | **5325** | **7600** | **14685** | **20175** |
| Net cash flow (a − b) | (325) | (1100) | (2685) | (7175) |
| Opening balance | | | (325) | (1100) |
| Closing balance | (325) | (1100) | (3010) | (8275) |

Seeing your income and expenditure itemised in this manner gives you a clear idea of budgetary requirements. Note that the terms on which you trade will have a direct effect on the cash flow of your business.

The headings of the model may differ according to the requirements of your business. From this example you will see arrangements for an additional cash injection will need to be made; perhaps a loan from your bank or other lender would be a viable option.

## *Notes on the cash flow forecast*

- **Receipts:** the money coming into your business. This will be mainly from sales once your business in established.

- **Payments:** all the money going out of your business. It will include payments to your supplier and capital or rental payments for cars or other equipment needed to run your business. All cash flow payments and receipts will be inclusive of VAT where applicable.

The term 'Working Capital' is used to describe the day-to-day financial resources used by your business for everyday trading purposes. They consist of:

- **Debtors:** customers to whom your have sold your goods or services on credit and who owe you money.

- **Cash:** the amount of money you have in your till, or deposited in your bank account.

- **Creditors:** the people you have bought from and now owe the price of your purchases.

- **Stock:** this depicts the value of materials purchased for re-sale, or materials to be transformed into finished objects.

Working capital needs to be carefully controlled so your enterprise can flourish.

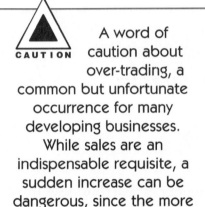

A word of caution about over-trading, a common but unfortunate occurrence for many developing businesses. While sales are an indispensable requisite, a sudden increase can be dangerous, since the more sales you make, the more money you need to purchase materials to support those sales.

Collecting the money due to you on time is important. Everyday a customer delays payment your profit margins are eroded, because of the time delay between the purchase of your materials, the time when they are sold, and the time the cash is actually received. Such a delay usually leads to a cash flow shortfall, a situation that can affect even those profitable businesses with full order books. It is vital to have enough cash at your disposal to meet these eventualities and thereby avoid the pitfalls of over-trading.

## Profit and loss forecasting

This forecast should contain information on your income and expenditure, similar to the previous forecast, except that the emphasis is on the profitability of your business. Forecasts usually cover a twelve-month period, but can be set at shorter intervals provided they are eventually collated to produce a yearly one. For periods exceeding a year, you'll need to complete a forecast for each annual period.

DEFINITION

> Income twenty shillings, expenditure 19 shillings and six pence
> – result – happiness.
>
> Income twenty shillings, expenditure 20 shilling and six pence
> – result – misery.
>
> (Mr. Micawber)

It is advisable to show items of expenditure in the months they were incurred. For example, rent for your business premises may only be paid quarterly. However, each quarterly payment represents rent for each month you occupy the building. Therefore, each quarterly bill should be divided by a third and allocated to each month of that quarter. The same procedure applies to telephone accounts and other similar items. The item of depreciation in the following Profit and Loss guide is a means of spreading the cost of machinery, vehicle, and other assets over the span of their useful lives.

For those of you who will be VAT registered, Value Added Tax does not need to be included in your profit and loss forecast. Normally it does not constitute a cost to your business.

> TIP
> Careful forecasting will help you to avoid any unexpected and harmful surprises.

If you expect to increase your sales, you must consider the effect this will have on the amount of working capital you will need. However, it should be included in your cash flow forecast. Profit and loss forecasts for your business plan normally take a complete overview of your business. Nevertheless, forecasts can be made on each product or service you offer. This will allow you to discard any unprofitable segment of your business.

Sample *Profit & Loss Forecast Guide*

## PROFIT & LOSS FORECAST GUIDE

### For DWR Software

### PERIOD June 2002 to May 2003

| RECEIPTS. | Month: June | | Month: July | |
|---|---|---|---|---|
| | Budget | Actual | Budget | Actual |
| Sales (net of VAT) (a) | 14500 | 12250 | 16500 | 17000 |
| **Less direct costs:** | | | | |
| Cost of materials | 9450 | 8150 | 10750 | 11000 |
| Cost of sales (advertising) | 800 | 750 | 1000 | 975 |
| **Gross profit (b)** | 4250 | 3320 | 4750 | 5025 |
| Gross profit margin (b/a $\infty$ 100%) | 29.3% | 27.1% | 28.8% | 29.5% |
| **Overheads:** | | | | |
| Salaries/National Insurance | 750 | 950 | 1800 | 2100 |
| Rent/Rates | 150 | 150 | | |
| Insurance | 75 | 80 | | |
| Repair & Renewals | | | 250 | 100 |
| Heating/Light/Power | | | 325 | 475 |
| Postage/Printing/Stationery | 1000 | 600 | | |
| Car/Travelling | | | | 60 |
| Telephone | | 85 | 100 | 140 |
| Professional fees | 400 | 400 | | |
| Interest charges | 75 | 110 | 150 | 200 |
| **Total overheads (c)** | 2450 | 2375 | 2625 | 3075 |
| Trading profit (b) – (c) | 1800 | 945 | 2100 | 1950 |
| Less depreciation | 150 | 125 | 150 | 125 |
| **Net profit before tax** | 1650 | 820 | 1950 | 1800 |
| Cumulative net profit | | | 3600 | 2620 |

To keep the above specimen as uncomplicated as possible 'Work in Progress' has been omitted. 'Work in Progress' is the term used to describe the value of work or stock in hand that has been completed but not sold. In some businesses, particularly in

> **note** A proportion of your home rent, or mortgage, as well as services like gas and electricity can be included if you work from home.

building and manufacturing, it can be an important part of the profit and loss forecast. This forecast can be adjusted for 'stock' or 'work in progress' by adding to the cost of materials the difference between the value at the beginning and at end of the period. This item should always be accounted for at cost. Your accountant can supply further advice on this topic.

## Notes on the profit and loss forecast

The definition of sales can be given as the value of stock sold and invoiced, regardless of whether payment has been received or not. Cost of materials is the actual cost, to you, of what you sell – whether you have paid for these items is not relevant. However, this cost of materials does not include one-off purchases such as a computer, nor would it appear elsewhere in this forecast, because it is regarded as part of your business's assets.

 Review your firm's overheads on a regular basis. Always look for ways to reduce costs.

Overheads will vary from business to business. If renting separate business premises, your rent plus the cost of rates and other expenses is to be included in your profit and loss report.

## *Understanding book-keeping*

Before you commence trading, you should take advantage of the book-keeping seminars organised by your local small business centre, particularly if your book-keeping experience is limited.

Although items in this section will not be used in your business plan, it is important to have a fundamental understanding of the subject. In the United Kingdom you are legally obligated to keep accurate records of all your business activities. An efficient system is an essential part of any well-run business. You will find it an indispensable aid in keeping your firm's finances under control.

An ideal book-keeping system for new or small businesses is to be found in *Book-keeping Made Easy* published by Law Pack Publishing Ltd. The book starts you off with a basic method of recording all your business transactions, and then takes you into the double entry methods as your business expands. Furthermore, it explains how to use the information stored within your financial records to your advantage.

If you have a computer, there are also many software packages available. In this section we will only deal with the cashbook and purchase ledger, the sales ledger and information about credit control are being handled separately.

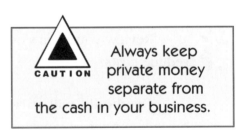

CAUTION Always keep private money separate from the cash in your business.

Maintaining accurate records will help you in many ways. Not only will you be able to meet your legal obligations, but you will also find it easier to complete your returns to the Inland Revenue (for Income tax purposes), not to mention your submissions to HM Customs and Excise for VAT.

You will also need to take data from these records to update your cash flow and profit and loss figures. By exercising control over your finances, you can reduce the workload of your accountant, which in turn will help him or her to reduce their bills.

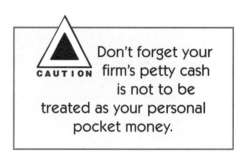

Don't forget your firm's petty cash is not to be treated as your personal pocket money.

Justifiable records are essential if your are going to monitor your performance and control your cash flow.

It is not difficult to keep accurate records, nor should it be time consuming. At first all you may need is a few folders in which you will need to retain:

- sales invoices to your customers (if retailing – cash or till receipts)

- purchase invoices from your suppliers

- bank statements

- petty cash receipts and purchase slips

This system will help you to keep everything in order and up to date. It will prove important when you go to the next stage and introduce book-keeping into the business. These records will not only allow you to keep track of the money coming in and going out, but will also provide instant information on how well you are doing financially.

The cashbook is the most important book for you to keep. It summarises your daily receipts and payments, and contains the method of payment and names of the parties concerned with each transaction. These transactions can be cash, cheque, standing order, direct debit or credit card. The left-hand pages of your cash book will record money coming in – sales, while the right hand pages will show the money you paid out – your purchases.

**SAMPLE CASH BOOK – RECEIPTS**

| Date (1) | Customer (2) | Item (3) | Bank (4) | Cash (5) |
|---|---|---|---|---|
| 9.6.00 | A. Greendale | Invoice 2103 | 450.00 | |
| 12.6.00 | Inland Revenue | Tax rebate | 150.00 | |
| 18.6.00 | D. Bird | Sale of van | 1750.00 | |
| 22.6.00 | J. Bond | Invoice 2098 | | 38.46 |
| 27.6.00 | P. Sterling | Deposit | | 250.00 |
| 2.7.00 | M. Cash | Invoice 2104 | 850.00 | |

Column (1) records the date of the cheque or cash was received. Column (2) & (3) notes the name of the customer paying you and the reason for the payment. The remaining columns denote whether or not the money has been banked or taken into petty cash.

**TIP** Employing a book-keeper either on a full or part time basis need not cost the earth. It will, however, leave you free to manage your business and avoid stress.

Now let us look at the payment side of your cash book.

**SAMPLE CASH BOOK – PAYMENTS**

| Date (1) | Supplier (2) | Item (3) | Bank (4) | Cash (5) | Materials | Wages/NI | Rent | Elec | Print | Phone | Trav |
|---|---|---|---|---|---|---|---|---|---|---|---|
| 2.6.00 | Br Tel | Chq 321 | 200 | | | | | | | 200 | |
| 5.6.00 | Reed Gar | Fuel | | 35 | | | | | | | 35 |
| 12.6.00 | P.O. | Stamps | 15 | | | | | | | 15 | |
| 14.6.00 | Sharp & Co | Chq 322 | 174 | | | | | | | 174 | |
| 18.6.00 | HH Prop | D/D | 380 | | | | 380 | | | | |
| 29.6.00 | D.Boy | Chq 323 | 865.45 | | 865.45 | | | | | | |

The items marked 1 to 5 records the movement of outgoing cash from your business, stating date, supplier and method of payment. The remaining columns provide an analysis of the types of expenses you are incurring. The number of columns required will depend on the nature of your business.

A purchase or bought ledger book will deal with all your purchases. It's advisable to have two folders – one for purchases paid and another for those unpaid. To simplify matters, a separate page should be used for each supplier. With this record book you can see at a glance what materials you purchase and whether or not you have paid for the goods in question.

*note* Paying your suppliers on time creates good business relationships. It will also ensure you'll always get good service.

Each bought ledger account should be headed with the supplier's name, address and telephone number. Always include the name of your contact and the credit limit you have been granted. On the right hand side enter details of all your purchases, along with:

- your order number

- date of order

- special instructions (if any)

- agreed delivery date

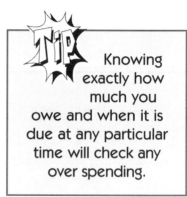

Knowing exactly how much you owe and when it is due at any particular time will check any over spending.

On the left-hand side of the account you must record each payment you make, noting the date and cheque number.

Total both columns each month. Subtract the amount you have paid from your total purchases. The sum remaining should reconcile with your suppliers' statement. To keep track of your purchases, always ensure you receive an invoice for your purchases and a receipt for any payments. Invoices should be kept in an unpaid folder in date order. When you send a cheque in payment of an invoice, note the date and cheque number on the invoice, in case of any future query. Now place the invoice in the invoice paid folder.

note

The manner in which you deal with your bought and sales ledgers shouldn't differ. The only distinction being one records what you owe, the other what is due to you.

## Sales ledger management

If you are a retailer dealing mainly with cash, a sales ledger will be of little use to you. However you will need to keep a summary of daily sales. Your cashbook, described earlier, can be easily adapted for this purpose. For many businesses, the sales ledger will be the most valuable asset – so manage it with care!

Your sales ledger will be arranged in exactly the same way as your purchase ledger, with one account per customer. The main difference between the two is that the sales ledger should contain the name of the person who pays your account, the name and position of the individual who accepts your deliveries, and the person who checks your invoice. This saves time when you need to chase for any outstanding sums due.

 To save time and money every month, do not send statements of account to customers with a zero balance. Send the remainder by first class post.

All sales should be recorded on the left-hand side of your ledger, and all payments received on the right. At the end of each month, add up each column by subtracting the money received from the sales. This will determine how much you are owed by each customer. A statement detailing the items sold to the customer and payments received should be sent each month to every customer, but before doing so you should check that your balances agree.

If a customer queries an order or invoice, always treat that complaint with urgency. Outstanding problems such as these are the most common reason for non-payment of an account.

To help you keep control of your sales, always issue an invoice. Invoices should be numbered in sequence and a copy retained for your folder. Copies of your customers' invoices should be kept in sales paid and unpaid folders, to be dealt with in the same manner as outlined in the purchase ledger section. Your terms of trade should be clearly displayed on all communications to

Sample *Invoice*

# PENNY STERLING TOYS

Unit 5, Nonsuch Industrial estate
Anytown Road,
Anytown WW11 XX22

Tel: 0000 000 000
Fax: 0000 000 001

Invoice No: 123456                              Date: June 7th 2000

To:

| | | |
|---|---|---|
| 1 Box | 12 assorted Jig-Saw puzzles @ £1.25p each | 15.00 |
| 3 Dozen | Yo-Yo's @ £9 per dozen | 27.00 |
| 4 Each | Playstations @ £125.60 each | 502.40 |

| | |
|---|---|
| Sub total: | 544.40 |
| VAT @ 17.5% | 95.27 |
| Total: | 639.67 |

**Credit Terms: 30 days from the date of invoice**

VAT Registration number: 987 6543 21

your customers, thus avoiding any misunderstanding about when you expect to be paid.

> **note**
> In an average business, 80% of outstanding debt is owed by only 20% of its customers. Chasing larger debts first improves your cash flow.

Keep a regular check on your unpaid invoices. Any overdue accounts should be chased persistently but politely. When contacting customers about unpaid accounts, always chase those customers who owe the largest amounts first. If you keep a routine check on outstanding sums due, you won't need to worry quite so much about its age.

Whilst it may not be possible to telephone all your customers each month to collect the money due to you, direct telephone contact is the best method to use particularly for your larger accounts. The smaller accounts should be contacted by a cycle of three or four letters, starting with a gentle reminder and finishing with a serious demand for payment. However, for the best effect, this letter cycle should be varied, or your customer will soon learn to delay payment until the final demand.

Late payment can have a devastating effect on the liquidity of small and start-up businesses. The British Institute's BS 7890 prompt payment code is aimed at improving payment practices in commerce, but this code will not stop bad debts from arising in the small business sector. Only the person with an invested

> **TIP**
> Never be afraid to ask your customer for the money owed to you. Otherwise, they will use you as a source of interest free credit.

interest in a prompt payment system will be able to enforce it successfully – so don't let your customers acquire the habit of late payment.

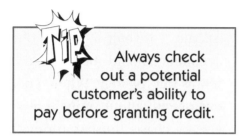

Always check out a potential customer's ability to pay before granting credit.

Within your sales ledger operation there should be an element of credit management. The aim of credit control is to eliminate the risk of bad debt as much as possible. Controlling credit also means obtaining bank and business references not only from new customers, but also from existing ones, at regular intervals. Beware – your customers' financial standing can change overnight, and it won't necessarily be a change for the better!

In addition, ensure your book-keeping system enables you to issue invoices promptly and indicates when they become overdue. Here are some other helpful hints:

- Clearly set out your terms of trading and do not deviate from them. Make sure customers are aware of these terms. Notify them of any changes the instant they occur.

- Keep clear and precise records. If you keep inaccurate accounts or invoices, your customers will have an excuse to delay paying you.

- Collect payments on time by establishing a collection pattern and sticking to it.

- If a customer promises to put a cheque in the post and it doesn't arrive, chase them for it again.

- If routine chasing does not produce results, stop further supplies to that customer as soon as it is viable to do so. Moreover, use the services of a reputable collection agency to resolve the situation.

## Summing up your finances

Having absolute control of your finances testifies to others that you are committed to the ultimate success of your business and lets them know that you can be relied upon to conduct your business in a professional manner. By making certain you will be paid on time, you ensure you have the cash to expand and enjoy your newly found prosperity.

## Promoting and selling your wares

1. **Direct Selling.** Please note: on May the 1st 1999, the new telecommunications regulations came into force. These directions are designed to protect consumers from receiving unsolicited sales calls and faxes, so proceed with caution if part of your sales campaign includes direct selling. If in doubt, obtain good legal advice before taking this approach.

2. **E-Commerce.** This fairly new and attractive way of promoting your business not only removes barriers that have prevented some small businesses from entering the field of their choice, but it also increases the geographical market place for both mass and niche products. Furthermore, it

> *note* Small business with an internet presence will always out-perform rivals who ignore this valuable market place.

allows small businesses to trade 24 hours a day around the world. Reports indicate that there are currently 100 million customers on line, with 3 joining every second – that's 260 thousand potential customers a day, if you choose to go online!

# Funding your business

# Chapter 5
## Funding your business

---

### What you'll find in this chapter:

- ⟹ How much do you really need?
- ⟹ Where to raise capital
- ⟹ Unconventional funding
- ⟹ Government aid and EU grants
- ⟹ Analysing your business funding

---

Traditionally, new businesses needing extra funding turn to the bank for an overdraft, forgetting that this arrangement is suitable only for short term use. Instead, new businesses should be planning to use the medium to long term finance terms that are really needed to get started. When borrowing money as a new business, you must be well prepared before approaching a potential lender – no matter what type of financial injection you are seeking for your business. Do you know at this stage what most lenders are looking for when they contemplate making an advance? You should. The main factors are:

1. **The owners.** Are they seen as credible, capable, competent and honest? Do they communicate effectively? Do they have a good track record in terms of employment, financial/business history? Do they have the skills, knowledge, experience and the right attitudes to make the business successful?

2. **Business plan.** Do they have a sound business idea? Are their forecasts reasonable, well thought out, and presented in a professional manner?

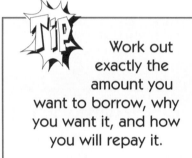

Work out exactly the amount you want to borrow, why you want it, and how you will repay it.

3. **Owners' financial investment.** How much of their own money are the owners putting into the business compared to the amount they wish to raise as loans? Depending on the economic climate and type of business, most banks prefer not to lend more than 50% of the total capital required, although this percentage may be increased due to government guarantees. These are dealt with later in this chapter. Don't fret if you haven't sufficient private funds to meet 50% of the investment. Go to the section on Government grants.

4. **Security.** It is easier to raise money and obtain a higher borrowing ratio if you have something of value to pledge against the loan. Preferred securities are those that can quickly be converted into cash in the event of default. Quoted shares, premium bonds, endowment policies and property that can be sold at auction are all considered as suitable security for loan purposes. Bear in mind that

your security – your home, if used – is at risk if you fail to meet the terms of the loan.

It is essential to build a firm, friendly alliance with your lenders. As most high street banks have business advisers to assist you in setting up your bank account, it shouldn't be too difficult to find one of these with whom you may develop a more complex relationship. By working together you can tackle challenges as they arise and resolve potentially 'difficult' situations before they become problems. Any foreseeable difficulties on the horizon could affect the way you meet your obligations, so tell your lender in advance, not when it's too late. Provided you keep your lender informed on a regular basis, telling them of good times as well as bad, you should find that they willingly listen and gladly assist you through any difficult patches you encounter.

## *How much do you really need?*

The amount you need to borrow depends on the shortfall you discovered when you produced your cash flow forecast. Deciding on the amount of money you will need to purchase equipment or premises is fairly easy. Determining the amount of money you'll need to cover gaps between your income and expenditure is a little more difficult. However, you don't have to rely on one finance house or bank. Each institution has facilities to meet different requirements, so perhaps a combination of lenders will prove right for you.

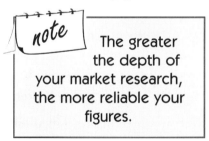

*note* The greater the depth of your market research, the more reliable your figures.

Although your forecast would have taken your projected sales and the trading terms of both your business and your suppliers into the equation, these figures are only estimates until you actually start trading. Slightly

When calculating the length of time you wish to repay the loan, don't forget to take into account seasonal sales patterns, such as Christmas.

overestimating your financial requirements must be better than having to go back to your banker, cap in hand, to ask for more cash within a short period of time.

Along with calculating the right amount of cash you need to borrow, you'll need to decide upon the right length of time for repaying any advance. A carefully construed cash flow plan will point out the peaks and troughs of your incoming and out going cash and answer this question.

## *Where to raise capital*

Again, the answer to this question depends on why your want the finance, so let's take a look at the varying financial institutions who are just waiting to lend you money.

1. **High Street Banks.** Normally the first port of call, the finance they offer embraces:

   • *Overdrafts.* These are mainly short term loans designed to provide stopgap funds to meet an unexpected shortfall, but are definitely not suitable as a replacement for long term capital. The main disadvantage is that the overdraft may have to be repaid on demand, so reliance on them should be avoided for anything other than short term use.

* *Credit cards.* While not an ideal way to finance your business, they can be useful for covering temporary cash flow problems. They would cover urgent stock purchase when faced with a sudden rush of sales, for instance. If you repay the facility when your

> *note* Before asking your bank for an overdraft to finance extra stock for a busy period such as Christmas, check with your suppliers. Some toy manufactures, for example, offer extended credit in the run up to the holiday.

account is received, the loan will be interest free, but prohibitive interest charges make the credit card unsuitable for long term use.

* *Loans.* These can provide long term working capital since they offer a suitable way to finance vehicles or other equipment. With a fixed rate loan, you will know what your repayments will be each month.

* *Mortgages.* Suitable for the purchase of freehold or long leasehold business premises, it is unlikely that a start-up business will want to take on this sort of commitment in it's embryo stage. Banks do offer other types of facilities through their subsidiary companies, therefore it is advisable to check with your local branch before committing yourself.

2. **Finance houses.** Finance Houses supply businesses with hire-purchase and contract rental agreements to acquire the use of vehicles and other equipment. The use of hire-purchase finance may

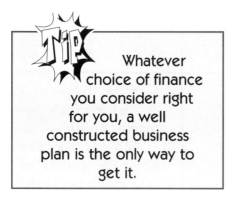

Whatever choice of finance you consider right for you, a well constructed business plan is the only way to get it.

be diminishing, but finance houses are replacing it with personal loans and contract purchase agreements. Factoring and discount houses provide off balance sheet finance for new and expanding businesses. They also supply finance for stock and raw materials as well as providing credit insurance.

3. **Venture Capital Firms.** While the principle aim of these firms is to provide start up capital, they tend only to consider established businesses. Although the current government has expressed its concern over this practice, most of the lending in this sector has been concentrated on management buy-ins and buy-outs. To obtain finance from this source your business must be trading as a limited company.

4. **Business Angels.** There are people with some business experience who want to invest in new firms and are prepared to take greater risks than normal financiers. The level of involvement these angels offer ranges from

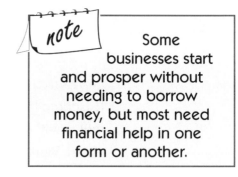

Some businesses start and prosper without needing to borrow money, but most need financial help in one form or another.

straightforward advice to the undertaking of non-executive directorships. While it is possible to have two or three business angels investing in one business, you should agree the level of commitment from the outset of negotiations.

5. **The Prince's Youth Business Trust.** In some cases, the trust will provide funds for young people, in addition to providing training, marketing support, counselling, and advice. More details of the trust can be found in Chapter 7.

6. **Credit Unions** are springing up throughout the country, and the fact unbeknown to many is that they offer micro/small business loans. Their maximum advance is restricted to £5,000 and repayment can be spread over three years - a handy sum for people starting out who need that little bit of extra cash to get their business off the ground.

7. **Community investment funds** represent an alternative source of borrowing for start-up businesses. There are currently over 150 funds established throughout the country. Not only do they lend to people who have been turned down by their banks but they offer top-up loans too. These funds are looking for a social return rather than a financial one so if you are going to be creating jobs in the area where a fund operates, you stand a good chance of funding. However, they will expect to get their money back eventually. Your local Chamber of Commerce can put you in touch with the nearest local community fund to you.

## *Unconventional financing*

In your every day life, you have probably come across bank and finance house loans, overdrafts, mortgages, and hire-purchase, so there is no need to discuss these matters further here. We shall go into a little more detail on leasing, factoring and stock financing, however, in order to help you learn about the right finance package for your enterprise. The financing discussed in this section will supplement any other form of borrowing you agree upon, but will not affect any overdraft or other loan arrangements you may have made.

## What a factor can do for you

CAUTION

> note
>
> For businesses buying goods from abroad: you'll need a letter of credit to avoid paying for goods before they are shipped. These letters of credit are issued by banks and are an internationally agreed method of payment.

There are two methods of factoring. The first, called invoice factoring, directly improves your cash flow. Instead of waiting the standard 30 days or more, money will be immediately advanced to you by a factor against the value of your invoices. Normally up to 80%, this figure is negotiable. The factor will then take over the management of your sales ledger collections. The other 20% (less the factoring fee and interest) is paid at agreed intervals. Invoice Factors offer bad bed protection by way of non-recourse deals, but at a price. Your forecasts will need to project sales of about £500,000 plus.

Some invoice factors augment their services by offering stock finance, which involves securing the value of your business stock. In doing so they can advance up to 100% of your suppliers' invoices, so you benefit from any special discounts on offer.

The second method is invoice discounting, which differs from the invoice factoring option in one major way. With the discounting option, you will retain the management of your sales ledger and the responsibility for collections, so if a customer doesn't pay or goes bust, you will have to reimburse the factor. These are mainly recourse deals.

# What leasing or contract hire can do for you

> *note*
>
> At the end of a lease contract the vehicle or equipment rented must be returned to the leasing company. These items cannot be retained by the hirer.

Principally, by using one of these options, you are given use of vehicles and equipment without having to tie up your capital. Although ownership of the equipment or motor vehicle remains with the finance house, rentals are tax deductible items – a distinct advantage. Clearly this option is a sensible method of financing for budgetary purposes. Contract hire is best used for vehicles, since maintenance agreements can be built-in. Rentals are kept low because the finance houses can reclaim the VAT levied at the time of purchase.

These types of finance have been classified as unconventional because they do not have to be listed in a firm's accounts.

# Finance for the small exporter

All major clearing banks in the UK operate small exporter finance schemes. Conveniently, they will not interfere with any other loan or financial arrangement you have put in place. The banks provide small businesses with cash at the time an export order is shipped, provided the correct export documentation has been lodged. Banks will advance up to 100% of the invoice value, less interest and a transaction fee. All small exporter programs require adequate credit insurance cover. Therefore, if your customer does not pay, you will not be required to reimburse the bank. All banks carry block insurance  cover arrangements, so you are saved from searching for suitable cover. Having credit insurance means lower interest charges for you.

Two other forms of non-recourse financing which are available to exporters and importers are:

- 'Forfaiting' involves bills of exchange, promissory notes or deferred letters of credit. In layman's terms, all of these are forms of IOUs. You discount these instruments to a forfaiting company and the risk of non-payment passes to

> note
>
> The discounting charges in respect of forfaiting and avalising must be included in your pricing policy (see Chapter 2). This also covers the costs for using the small exporter schemes.

them. Because these bills vary between 90/180 days, it is not unknown for them to pass from one forfaiting company to another. Forfaiting is for exporting use.

- 'Avalising' is a simple form of a bill of exchange, allowing you to import goods from an overseas supplier on extended credit terms not normally on offer. Avalising is a form of guarantee; to aval is to endorse a bill of exchange or promissory note. If the term 'Bills of Exchange' appears confusing, don't worry, it is only a document that promises to pay the named recipient an agreed sum of money on a certain date, like a cheque. Should you commence exporting at any time, go along to your local bank. They will gladly explain the procedures.

## Government aid and EU grants

Regrettably, there are no longer any universal grants on offer, but there are some that could be available to you, depending on the type of business

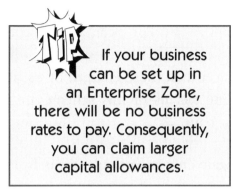

If your business can be set up in an Enterprise Zone, there will be no business rates to pay. Consequently, you can claim larger capital allowances.

being conducted and its location. Currently, there are only six enterprise zones in the UK, although there are other places designated as 'Assisted Areas'. If you located your business in an inner city area or one of the poorer regions which fall into the category of "Assisted Areas", you could qualify for any available grants. For more information on assisted areas, contact the DTI's web site at www.dti.gov.uk

Selective regional assistance gives grants of up to 15% of the start-up costs of a project. In some areas you can get assisted grants for marketing and export. Contact your local council, Chamber of Commerce or Business Link centre for up-to-date information on grants.

The Government Guarantee Loan Scheme comes into operation when the level of your personal investment falls below the bank's underwriting criteria. However, your business plan will only be forwarded for inclusion in this scheme at your specific request, i.e., if you ask for your loan application to be dealt with in this fashion. A government department would then study your business plan and if viable, the government would guarantee up to 80% of your business loan.

If you follow through with this option, an additional interest charge would be made, but if this is the only way your business can get off the ground, it is probably well worth the extra cost. Banks are in business to lend money, so if your idea is sound and well presented they will not hesitate to provide the funds you need.

An alternative to the above grant is the European Investment Bank, which is supported by the Government. It works in conjunction with high street banks. Their interest rates are lower than those charged by usual banks and there terms are also less stringent. Details of this scheme are readily available from the local branch of your bank.

EU grants are also available, but again only in particular areas. By locating your business in the right area, grants of up to £750 can be available from the European Regional Development fund. You will need to check with your local council to learn if any are in partnership with Business Link. Alternatively, if yours is a firm with less than six employees, contact your local small business centre.

Many Business Links subscribe to a grant-finder database. They will search through this database for you for a nominal fee.

Finally, if your business is of a technical or innovative nature the Department of Trade and Industry offer 'Smart Grants'. These grants are available towards the cost of feasibility and/or technical studies. Up to 75% of the cost can be obtained, plus up to 30% of development costs.

There are many other local grants on offer – one might be suitable for you. Keep in touch with your local Business Link or small business centre for the most up-to-date information, since new initiatives are constantly being developed to help people just like you. Read the business pages of the daily and Sunday newspapers; they'll keep you abreast of current developments in your region.

## *Analysing your business funding*

Before approaching any lender make sure you have considered every angle and know what financial arrangement is best for your business. When meeting with a potential lender or investor, be confident. Be able to say how much funding you will need, what use it will be put to, how long you will want

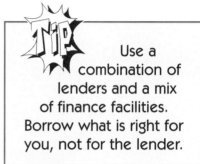

this funding to last. Armed with this material, a good business idea, and a well thought out business strategy, your business should get off the ground in next to no time.

# Structuring your business plan

6

# Chapter 6
## Structuring your business plan

By now you should be fully aware of the knowledge and the resources you will need to achieve your ambitions in your chosen field of business. In addition, you probably know which assets you lack, but you'll also know where and how to acquire them. Now is the time to put all those facts and figures your have been gathering into a formal report, one which you can use to measure the performance of your business.

You may know precisely what you want to do and how you are going to accomplish your plans, but unless this information is written down and presented in a professional manner, your ideas won't get a second glance.

> **note** Some people start a business and prosper without any plan at all, but for every firm that does get by without planning, many more fail.

Outsiders will demand to see your every move – in precise black and white terms. Your business plan will tell them in minute detail just how you will attain sufficient profitable sales to make your efforts worthwhile. Hopefully, your business ideas will develop continuously. As they do, write them down. If you can think of the consequences of each step and mould these ideas until they are just right for you, then you will always be ahead of the game. Don't ever think that concepts must be discarded because they proved to be unworkable. As you expand they may be adapted or re-thought into profitable notions.

The more homework you do before actually starting your business, the better. You'll stand less risk of failure if you don't rush into it prematurely. Once you are confident that your preparation is complete, you can start setting out your stall, by way of a business plan.

## Why you need a business plan

The importance of having a business plan has been continuously stated throughout this book, yet it cannot be stressed enough. Think of it as your business's CV, but instead of asserting your achievements, it advertises your ambitions and the solid business methods you will use to attain your goals.

> **note** A business plan should not be used just to obtain finance and start your business - it is also a valuable management tool that needs to be reviewed from time to time.

As time goes by, you will be able to see whether the business is performing to expectation. If it is not, you will be able to modify your methods and bring your business back to a profitable route. Bringing all the information together will give you an integrated picture of how your business will work and will help you avoid the many common pitfalls of running a business.

Drawing up your firm's plan you will ensure that you have:

- confirmed the business is viable

- identified strengths and weaknesses and developed improvements

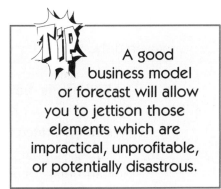

A good business model or forecast will allow you to jettison those elements which are impractical, unprofitable, or potentially disastrous.

- targets by which you can measure your success

- a coherent picture of your aims and how these will be achieved

- the opportunity to discover different 'what if' scenarios without risk

- a presentation document for fund raising

## *Basic ingredients*

All business modules share common characteristics; they cover one-to-three year trading periods, they disclose how your business is expected to perform and they demonstrate the following:

- details of your product or service

- the type of business

- details of main suppliers and costs

- marketing, operational and financing plans

- key personnel

- how the business will develop

Once you have completed your business plan, you should have answered these four key questions with a degree of confidence:

- Will people buy my product or service?

- Can I produce or provide it?

- Can I make money at it?

- Can I finance the project?

Now let's see how a business plan should look, in order to have the maximum effect. A case study and specimen business plan that you can adapt for your own use is to be found at the end of this book.

## Constructing your business plan

Apart from the details mentioned in the last segment in the front cover of your plan will identify:

- the name, address, telephone, fax and Internet address (if you have one) of your business

- the period the plan covers

- capital structure

- when trading will start or when it began (if already trading)

The capital structure shows in brief whose money has been put into the business. Unless the business is up and running, however, it will be the owner(s). The wording will depend upon the form your trading will take. A sample of the distinct variations follows.

(a) **Sole trader.** If you are trading on your own give the name of the owner (i.e. yourself) and any trading name you have adopted, plus the amount you are personally investing, and include the value of any equipment you are bringing to the business. For instance:

| Owner's name | Capital invested (£) |
|---|---|
| Penny Sterling | 10,000 |

During this section you may find it helpful if you turn to the case study intermittently to see how this data fits in.

(b) **Partnership.** Partnership details should be given in the same manner as a sole trader. For example:

| Partner's name | Capital invested (£) |
|---|---|
| Penny Sterling | 5,000 |
| Mark Cash | 5,000 |

(c)  **Limited company.** This differs slightly from the previous two forms of business. Give the name of each person and indicate whether they are a director or shareholder (in a new business they are almost always both), the number and value of ordinary shares they hold and the percentage held. Also show any loans each individual has made to the business. This is illustrated thus:

| Name | Shareholder | Director | No. of shares | Nominal value | % total | loans to business |
|---|---|---|---|---|---|---|
| Penny Sterling | yes | yes | 25 | £1 | 50 | 2,500 |
| Mark Cash | yes | yes | 25 | £1 | 50 | 2,500 |

Be sure to include all directors and major shareholders. Instead of a chart, you may prefer to write a brief paragraph on each company member and officer.

(d)  **Co-operatives (Unlimited and Limited).** These are more or less the same as a partnership. For an unlimited co-operative the amount invested will be shown as capital invested. For a limited one it will be stated as loans to business.

When planning your business, ponder every aspect seriously. Then think hard, think long and then think again.

| Members names | Capital invested (£) |
|---|---|
| Penny Sterling | 5,000 |
| Mark Cash | 3,000 |
| Peter Franc | 2,000 |

The different forms of trading mentioned above are covered in greater detail, along with their advantages and disadvantages, in the following chapter.

DEFINITION

Mission statements are best described as a vision statement. Whilst personal objectives are not normally included in a business plan, there is no reason why they cannot be recorded. The purpose of the statement is to

remind you what you want out of the business. Make sure your business aims take into account your personal objectives, but beware, sometimes business growth cannot be achieved without sacrificing personal goals.

It's up to you to live up to the vision. You will need to communicate this vision to everyone working for the organisation. The mission statement also needs to convey that you are good at what you do. A typical mission statement might state:

'To provide the best customer service, through well trained, competent, motivated and happy staff." Or "Constantly being the best run garage in Manchester, run by people who care.'

A mission statement sets the scene against which the business objectives can be established. These objectives will give direction and targets to your business. They should also help you to resolve short term problems. The definition of your business objectives is the most important thing, enabling you to keep track of where you are going and how you will get there!

> *note*
>
> Long term objectives can be achieved by setting a series of short term targets. The targets should initially be set for a year, then for subsequent years to help you stay on target.

For the first year of your business plan your business targets need to be set under separate headings, such as:

### Financial

1. To obtain a return on investment of 15% before tax.
2. Achieve net profits of £50,000 per annum.

### Marketing

1. Reach sales of £80,000 per month.
2. Increase customer base by 5 new customers per month.

### Operations

1. Maintain machine operation at 85% of working time.
2. Produce 20 units per hour at a cost of £9.50 per unit.

CAUTION Don't try and be clever by papering over any cracks in your business plan. If your scheme isn't foolproof it won't take an experience financier long to see through it.

## *Practical steps to get you started*

As you go through each stage of your business planning put all your findings down on paper. You may find that some of the data you have collected is of little or no use to you, but it is always better to have too much information than too little.

It does not matter in which order you collect your information. Nevertheless, it is important that the report provides an honest picture of your intentions and ambitions. Moreover, it needs to be submitted in a logical order to avoid any confusion forming in the mind of a possible lender or investor.

In the event you are unsure of any part of your business plan, seek the advice of an accountant or similar professional before submitting it.

A well designed letter heading and business logo are invaluable to a new business. Go to a little extra expense, it will be worth it!

Decide on a trading name, and if possible, select your business premises before writing your business plan, but do not commit to anything until you are sure you have all finances in place. If the premises do get taken before you are ready, your plan can easily be altered.

Now go to the appendix, and see for yourself what a feasible business plan should look like.

## Business plan digest

Talk to all those who will be involved in your business. Note their ideas and listen closely to any doubts that might be expressed. Present your business plan clearly and precisely. Tell it as it is, warts and all.

# Tax and other things

7

# Chapter 7

## Tax and other things

Someone once said 'only two things are certain in life – death and taxes'. Happily, we shall not be discussing the former in detail. Unfortunately, we do have to mention taxes. You must make provision for tax and insurance. Tax demands have the habit of popping through your letterbox when your cash flow is at it's lowest, and they have to be paid no matter what state your finances are in. Likewise, insurance; if a disaster that isn't covered strikes your business, you'll soon be shutting up shop.

Everyone is liable to pay Income tax and National Insurance, whether a sole trader, a partner or director of a company. These two, together with Corporation and Inheritance tax, are called direct taxation. If your business

> **TIP** The cost of advice from an accountant or tax specialist could be more than covered by the savings in time and money they recommend.

turnover exceeds a certain level (check current level with HM Customs and Excise), VAT must be levied on your goods or services. VAT and stamp duty are classified as indirect taxation. Let's take a glance at the taxes you might have to pay.

- **Income tax.** Operating as a sole trader means you will pay the normal rates of Income tax on the whole of your profits, not your level of drawings. If you operate as a partnership the amount of income tax charged to your profits will depend on the income tax rates paid by the individual partners on their incomes. Personal allowances are unaffected.

- **National Insurance.** A self-employed person is liable to pay Class 2 National Insurance Contributions unless your earnings are extremely low. Class 4 contributions may also be due if your net profits exceed a specific

> **note** The moment you start planning your business, contact all your local Revenue agencies, they will send details of the current rates of taxes and allowances.

level (for current levels, contact your local Contributions Agency). You will be obliged to deduct National Insurance contributions from salaries paid to all employees.

- **VAT (Value Added Tax).** Subject to a minimum threshold, you must register your business for VAT purposes. Not all goods and services are subject to the maximum rate. Some are zero rated, while others are exempt and still others have a lower tariff. It is important to be fully aware of the VAT regulation relating to your business. A number of leaflets are available free of charge from your local VAT office.

- **Capital Gains tax.** This is a tax on capital profits made on items like investments and land. Capital Gains tax becomes due if you sell such items for more than you paid for them, after allowing for inflation. Any capital losses

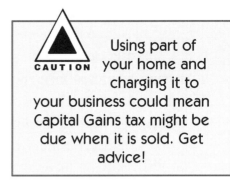

Using part of your home and charging it to your business could mean Capital Gains tax might be due when it is sold. Get advice!

arising from the sale of an asset can be offset against any gain.

- **Inheritance tax.** This is paid on the value of a deceased estate, at the date of death. This includes property, shares and other personal assets. Any assets transferred to other ownership less than seven years before death are also included. There is a level below which no tax is due. Your accountant will tell you the current figure.

- **Corporation tax.** This is a tax paid on the profits made by a limited company. Profit is defined as being the total sales less allowable expenses, plus investment income. By increasing allowable expenses the director can reduce

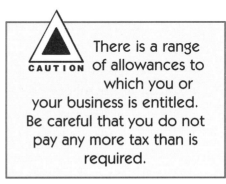

There is a range of allowances to which you or your business is entitled. Be careful that you do not pay any more tax than is required.

the amount of corporation tax paid, as well as pension

contributions for themselves and their staff. Accurate book-keeping records will ensure your accountant takes into account every expense which can be off-set.

## Insurance

Protecting your business by having adequate insurance cover not only makes sense, but in some circumstances is also compulsory by law. After all, your business could be the only source of income for you and

Did you know it is possible to insure against the loss of key staff due to illness?

your dependants. Faced by a sudden claim for damages from a customer, or a situation where your enterprise can no longer function because of a fire, how would your business be revived without the benefits of insurance? Furthermore, customers lost during a time of inactivity might never be recovered. Therefore, it is highly advisable that you consult a reputable insurance broker to make sure you get the right insurance programme to cover your business.

## Compulsory insurance

- **Public liability** will protect you against legal action taken by members of the public (not employees) that arise from your business activities. Whilst this is not really a compulsory item it's placed here, at the top of the list, to stress how vital this cover is.

- **Employers liability.** If you employ people other than your family you are legally required to take out employer's liability cover. This protects you against claims from employees that arise from injury or death sustained at work or in the course of their employment.

- **Engineers plant policies or contracts.** Inspection of certain types of plant and equipment by a competent person is mandatory. Non-compliance could mean complete shut-down of your operation. An annual inspection contract or policy is required to be in force to comply with these regulations.

- **Motor insurance.** Current legislation specifies it is compulsory to have third party liability insurance on all motor vehicles scheduled in the road traffic act. Company vehicles that are an asset of your business need to be

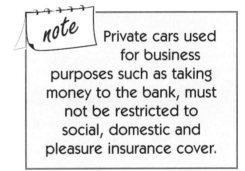

*note* Private cars used for business purposes such as taking money to the bank, must not be restricted to social, domestic and pleasure insurance cover.

covered against material damage by comprehensive cover.

## Non-compulsory insurance

Don't skimp on cover simply because the following types are not compulsory. Remember, it is your assets and livelihood that are at risk.

- *   **Material Damage insurance.** If leasing your business premises, covering the building may be part of the contract. This cover should also include stock and equipment against such perils as fire, flood, storm, burst pipes and other specified causes.

> **note** The types of insurance shown here are just some of the main types of cover available. Confer with your insurance broker and check on your insurance needs regularly.

* **Product liability.** This will provide cover for any legal liability arising from claims against you from members of the public for bodily injury or damage to their property from goods supplied, serviced, tested, or repaired by you or your staff.

* **Loss of Profits.** In the event your business premises are unusable as a result of an insured peril, a fire for example, the income of the business will be maintained as if the disaster had not occurred.

* **Goods in Transit.** Motor vehicle policies do not normally cover goods in a vehicle. This policy would cover goods being delivered to customers either in your own vehicles or sent by any other means.

* **Professional indemnity** offers cover for legal liability for professional errors and omissions made while carrying out your business. It will also cover those working for you.

* **Pensions.** A pension scheme will provide a tax efficient fund to provide income in retirement, thereby reducing long term dependency on your business.

> **TIP** If there is a trade association for the type of business you operate, enquire about any special insurance cover they've negotiated. Premiums may be cheaper.

Details of your current insurance coverage and any other types of insurance you are considering should be noted in your business plan.

# Forms of trading

Before you commence trading you need to consider the legal form your business will take, although the type of business you will be operating will have some influence on your decision. Each classification has its advantages and disadvantages. The salient points are summarised below:

- **Sole trader.** This is exactly what it sounds like. Someone who owns and runs a business as an individual; the ultimate responsibilities will rest with him or her. Any profit made belongs to the sole trader. You simply decide to start trading and off you go. You should tell the Inland Revenue you have started trading as a self-employed person.

There is no need to register a business name, but you cannot trade in the name of somebody who is already trading. Words such as Royal and Institute require special permission. Read the booklet 'Business Names – Guidance Notes' available free from the Companies Registration Office, Cardiff.

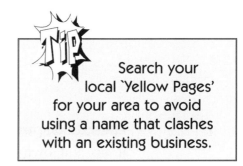

Search your local 'Yellow Pages' for your area to avoid using a name that clashes with an existing business.

| | |
|---|---|
| **Advantages** | easy to set up |
| | few legal implications |
| | one person ownership |
| **Disadvantages** | If the business fails you could lose everything you own. You are also personally liable for your employees actions. |

- **Partnerships.** A number of people who pool their resources and knowledge into a single business in which they are joint owners. When forming a partnership it is worth considering a 'Partnership Agreement'. This is not a sign of distrust but simply a document setting out who invests what, and how profits are to be shared, not forgetting details of each partners duties and responsibilities. Every partner is deemed jointly and severally liable. This means you are responsible both collectively and individually for the business debts, even if they were not incurred by you.

  | | |
  |---|---|
  | **Advantages** | somewhat easy to set up |
  | | many heads are better than one |
  | | fewer legal implications than a company |
  | **Disadvantages** | You are held responsible for your partners commercial decisions. |
  | | You must pay the partners share of the business debts if they do not pay. |

- **Limited Company.** This legal identity is separate from those who set it up and own the shares. A limited company is owned by its shareholders and directors are appointed to run it. In a small business it is likely the directors and shareholders are the same. In a limited company you must issue a minimum of two shares and appoint two directors, one of which must be the company secretary. The directors of a small company could be husband and wife. A Company Secretary is responsible for ensuring all legal obligations are met.

  | | |
  |---|---|
  | **Advantages** | Greater opportunity to raise finance |
  | | liability is limited, you are not responsible for the company's debts. |

**Disadvantages**   more costly to set up and run

must disclose details of business and accounts

legal requirements to fulfil

A Limited Partnership vehicle is not generally used these days for running a business, although charities do make good use of them.

Directors who are fraudulent or allow the company to trade when it's insolvent can be personally liable for the company's debts – Insolvency Act 1986.

Another trading form is the Co-operative, again rarely seen, apart from the local Co-ops and building societies we all know and love. The advantages and disadvantages of using this form are the same as limited companies and partnerships, with additional drawbacks such as:

- returns are not based upon the level of financial investment

- all members have equal voting rights, rights which are not based on the level of share ownership

note Care is needed when buying a franchise. Make sure you investigate it thoroughly. If you believe over optimistic projections without conducting your own research, you run the risk of failure.

- return on money invested is limited

Franchising is becoming an increasingly popular way to start a business. This option allows you to operate a business using an established format. A franchiser grants you the right to use their trade name, product or service. They also provide back-up support and management skills. In return you invest time, effort and money. A franchiser has a vested interest in your success, so using this format can be less risky than going it alone. Many of the high street banks have set up special departments to deal with franchises.

All you need to ask yourself now is, 'What type of business will I be running?'

## *Help and advice*

At first it must seem a frustrating and overwhelming task; putting together a business takes an enormous amount of time and effort. Fortunately, there is always a light at the end of the tunnel. There are people and organisations ready and willing to help and offer advice. All you have to do is ask them to help.

Never put off asking for advice and always seek it earlier rather than later. This will help you to avoid making costly mistakes and stop you from going broke. Apart from the organisations mentioned in various parts of this book, don't forget friends and family. Following this chapter you

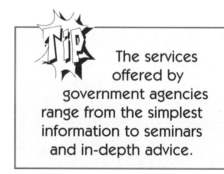

The services offered by government agencies range from the simplest information to seminars and in-depth advice.

will find a list of useful websites, which are overflowing with help and advice, use them as often as you need.

There will be times when you'll need help from professional advisers such as accountants and solicitors. These will charge you a fee, and they are not cheap. However, most professional advisers usually offer a free preliminary interview. Use this period to assess if they are the right solicitor or accountant for you. Ask for details of their charges, and again haggle.

Banks are also convenient sources of advice, but they can be biased in relation to the services they offer, so beware. Furthermore, they will charge for providing this service and sometimes their costs are not always clear.

There is also a range of government backed initiatives aimed at those new to commerce. Although each service has its own area of operation, they do work in partnership with each other. Each of the three services mentioned can be found in you local telephone directory, or contacted through the Department of Trade and Industry on 020 7215 5000. Website address: www.dti.gov.uk.

When in the process of starting-up a business, turn to your local small business centre. Such centres, supported by major business organisations, offer impartial and confidential advice without charge. Please note that while some types of business training is offered free of charge, others will have a small cost. You should contact the small business centre in the area your business will be located, not in the area where you live.

For the established business with ten or more employees, Business Links offers the best package. Their goal is to support firms on the brink of expansion and they achieve this goal by providing each company with a team of Business Advisers, specialists either in a particular subject or with special knowledge of

Business Links may provide training and advice on a variety of subjects from IT to Exporting, in addition to their free consultations.

certain business sectors. Website address: www.businesslink.co.uk

Training and Enterprise Councils (TECs) run business start-up schemes aimed at the unemployed who wish to start their own business. In certain areas, financial support, grants and loans on special terms may be available. To find out more about your local TEC, contact the National Federation of Enterprise Agencies on 01234 354055 . Website address: www.nfea.com

The Forum for Small Businesses is an independent enterprise offering a platform for the small business community to air their grievances by lobbying the government. Membership also provides a number of other benefits. Telephone 01565 634467 or fax 01565 650059 for more information.

The Chambers of Commerce are the national voice of business. They provide a varied range of commercial services with member discounts. For details of your local Chamber, contact the British Chambers of Commerce on 020 7565 2000.

The Prince's Youth Business Trust is probably the largest start-up agency in the voluntary sector. It helps young unemployed people and those of limited means. Young people from ethnic minorities, people with disabilities, and young ex-offenders are all welcome. Would-be entrepreneurs will need to have a good business idea and be able to demonstrate commitment and enthusiasm. To contact the Prince's Trust, telephone 020 7543 1234 or 0141 248 4999 if you live in Scotland. Website address: www.princes-trust.org.uk

## Other handy contact numbers

In general, the first point of contact for anyone seeking information is the telephone. It's fast, and telephoned requests for printed information are usually dealt with on the same day. Therefore, only the telephone numbers of the following organisations have been given here:

- **British Standards Institute** supply itemised information on all British standards, in particular payment standards and BS ISO 9000. Telephone 020 8996 9000 with your enquiries. Website address: www.bsi.org.uk

- **Chartered Institute of Marketing**, for sales, marketing and related information, and details on seminars and recruitment issues. For all enquiries telephone 01628 427500. Website: www.cim.co.uk

- **Registrar of Companies**, Companies House, holds records of all limited companies and will provide leaflets on directors obligations, filing annual returns and accounts. For assistance ring 01222 380801. Website: www.companies-house.gov.uk

- **Department of Trade** provides data for importers and exporters. Importers should contact 01642 364 333, or fax 01642 533 557. Exporters can obtain information by telephoning 020 7215 8070, or faxing 020 7215 8564. Website: www.dti.gov.uk

- **Health and Safety Executive**, for details about safety in the workplace. Telephone 08701 545500. Website: www.hse.gov.uk

- **Institute of Directors** offers free practical business information for its members. Assists small businesses in all aspects of starting a business. General enquiries can be made by dialling 020 7730 4600. Website: www.iod.co.uk

- **Office of Data Protection Registrar**. For all data protection registration requirements call 01625 545 754. Website: www.dpr.gov.uk

- **Office of Fair Trading** (Consumer Credit Licensing Branch) If you are to offer non-trade customers any form of consumer finance, you are required to obtain a consumer credit licence. For details telephone 020 7211 8000, or fax 020 7211 8800. Website: www.oft.gov.uk

- **Patent Office** for tangible help to protect your designs, trademarks and inventions. Simply dial 08459 500 505. Website: www.patent.gov.uk

# *List of other useful websites for entrepreneurs*

### Accounting & credit

www.acca.co.uk/index.html - the Association of Chartered Accountants

www.icm.org.uk - for information on credit management

### Business advisers

www.iba.org.uk - for those of you seeking professional business advisers

www.nfea.com - another site for business advisers

### Finance

www.anbusiness.com - direct source of start-up loans

www.MBNALoans.co.uk - for business finance

www.factors.org.uk - Factors and Discounters Association

www.fla.org.uk - Finance and Leasing Association

### Franchising

www.british-franchise.org.uk - for advice on franchising

### General business

www.smallbiz.uk.com - small business directory

www.e-ethniconine.com - information site for ethnic businesses

www.bt.com/getstarted - for easy to understand advice for new businesses

www.businesszone.co.uk - ideal for locating resources

www.startinbusiness.co.uk - tips for running your own business

### Legal

www.justask.org.uk - most of the information available is free

www.compactlaw.co.uk - provides access to basic legal documents and advice

### Personnel

www.jobsworth.com - useful site for downloading employment contracts

**Research**

www.cbi.org.uk - a priceless source of information

www.cima.org.uk - Chartered Institute of Management

## *Time to recollect*

A lot of the help and advice you will need is obtainable free of charge. Make time to talk to anybody who can assist you. Constantly refer to the respective chapters of this book if you are unsure where to turn.

# Appendix
## Case study and sample business plan

## Case study – Sales Ledger Services

### Introduction

Mike Cunningham was employed as a credit manager for the last six years with a trade finance company. Due to a recent merger, he was offered an attractive redundancy package. Having toyed with the idea of setting-up his own business for a couple of years, he thought this was an opportunity not to be missed.

Using the knowledge he gained over the preceding years, Mike plans to set up a business as a Sole Trader by establishing 'Sales Ledger Services' (SLS), a new business service aimed at small and medium sized firms. He has chosen to rent office accommodation in an office complex near to the town centre, which has ample car parking, as well as facilities for his clients and staff. It is convenient to all major road networks, offering easy access to the nearby towns and industrial estates, thus enlarging the catchment area for increasing his client base. Mike decided to prepare his business plan for one year and intends to commence trading on 1st September.

## Mission statement and business objectives

Mike believes in using well-trained staff who will be eager to provide a quality service and to take extra care of his clients. His primary targets are to establish the business and take drawings of £15,000 in the first year. In this first year, he anticipates making a loss of about £3,000. In the second year, he aims to increase his drawings to £20,000 and produce profits of £30,000.

## Capital and personal circumstances

Mike has £5,000 savings, the redundancy payment of £10,000 and a car, valued at another £5,000, which he is putting into the business. He is married with a teenage daughter. Mike's wife does not work at present but she's agreed to help out part-time. Her wages have been included in the first years' drawings. National Insurance and Income tax will also be paid from the drawings.

## Key employees

In the beginning, apart from Mike and his wife, there will be one full-time employee. He calculates that within two months another full time and possibly a further two part-time staff will be required. The initial staff will be:

- **Mike Cunningham**, the owner, 40 years of age. A Fellow of the 'Institute of Credit Management', he has worked as an accounts clerk, a credit controller, a supervisor covering all aspects of credit control and in management. In the past he has worked for manufacturing and service industries, in medium and large firms.

Mike's knowledge and experience includes both manual and computer sales ledger accounting systems.

- **Linda Cunningham**, aged 34 years old. Linda hasn't worked since their daughter was born, but she is a trained book-keeper and is arranging to go on a refresher course, which also covers computerised accounting.

- **Karen Swift**, a credit control supervisor, is 28 years old. Karen spent a number of years as an accounts clerk with a leasing company before leaving to work with Mike as a credit control trainee. Quickly promoted, they worked as a team, reducing the level of outstanding debt. Unhappy with her new employers she plans to join Mike in this endeavour.

## *Marketing*

Sales Ledger Services plans to operate initially within a twenty-five mile radius of its offices, with information supplied by the local Business Link. Mike discovered there are nearly 3,750 small businesses in his area. In addition, about 1,400 start up every quarter and about 1,200 close within that period. The main reason given for the closures were inadequate financial controls. He hopes his service will mean fewer closures for these businesses.

Mike's market research was conducted by post and telephone. He purchased a mailing list comprising small and medium sized businesses from the local Business Link and targeted firms with less than 20 employees in the manufacturing and service sectors. The information he obtained supplied him with enough data to confirm his idea was viable.

Mike next compiled a questionnaire and sent it, along with a reply paid envelope and covering letter explaining the service he proposed, to 200 prospective clients. He used the same questionnaire to telephone a further 100 business people. Within the body of the questionnaire he asked:

Would you be interested in further details of this service?

Is there a similar service you would like to see offered?

It was made clear that only those who indicated their interest by responding to the questionnaire would be bothered again. The covering letter and telephone call were both finished by thanking the people for their time.

Mike discovered from the telephone research that 14% requested further details of his service, 8% stated they would be interested in a book-keeping service and 5% suggested a pay-roll service. A further 2% requested details of all three services.

The response to the postal survey was not as impressive. Only 48% replied, and of these, only 9% required more details. Another 4% suggested the pay-roll services and 1% the book-keeping services. No one requested all three.

From this research, Mike realised he had a possible forty clients for his sales ledger service, but by adding book-keeping and pay-roll to his services, he knew a further twenty possible clients could be added. Mike hoped that these customers might be persuaded to use his other service later on and realised that by introducing these other services, his client list would not be restricted just to business-to-business clients.

Another thing Mike learned through his research is that word of mouth is clearly the best way to promote a business. Until the business was established, Mike would have to rely on direct mailing, telephone and personal calling. He is hoping his local paper might carry an article on his new venture in their business pages. A promotion budget of £4,000 has been allocated.

His major competitors for the sales ledger service would be factoring companies. While these would have the advantage of offering clients cash for their invoices, Mike felt the personal service and system of credit control he was offering would improve his client customers' payment habits. Therefore, the need for supplying his clients with up front cash would be eliminated. In fact, smaller firms preferred Mike's personal on-site service; they felt more comfortable with their sales ledger operation being kept in-house. Mike also faced competition from other book-keeping and pay-roll agencies, as well as accounting practices, but his prime service gave him the edge over his rivals.

## Premises

Unsure of the size of the office accommodation he would eventually require, Mike agreed to rent a 500 square foot office in a seedbed centre. This had the added advantage of having some small business clients close by. The rental was agreed for the first 6 months, but must be re-negotiated on a monthly basis thereafter. This would allow Mike to expand his business without having to move location. Being newly built premises and with carpets included, little fitting out was required, except for desks, chairs and any furniture required for a small reception area.

## Materials

Apart from a continuing supply of advertising brochures, letter headings, invoices and business cards, no other supplies are envisaged.

## Staffing

Mike and Karen will be the two 'full-time' employees. However, to deal with the immediate staffing needs, Mike will have to recruit two part-time employees straight away - an experienced book-keeper and a pay-roll clerk. In the meantime, Linda will breach the gap.

## Equipment

A telephone and fax have already been installed. Desks, filing cabinets, chairs etc., would be purchased at auction. £2,000 has been set aside for good quality furniture. Two desk-top computers would be a necessity, together with two lap-tops, so it was decided to lease these items at £160 per month. The sales ledger software would be purchased 'off the shelf' and modified. Standard book-keeping and pay-roll systems would be used.

## Transport

Mike's car, a Rover 600, would be transferred to the business and the running costs for would be paid by the business. An adjustment will be made to his income tax because of the benefit he'll enjoy. The decision to employ only those people who had access to a motor vehicle was made. As Karen and any of these new staff members would be required to use their cars for business, a mileage allowance of 25p per mile would be paid.

## Insurance

The staff will be expected to modify their own motor insurance. Property insurance for the office is included in the rent. Mike will take out a contents policy, as well as obtaining Public and Employers liability cover. Loss of profit and professional indemnity are also considered a must. Through his insurance broker he is arranging for the £2,400 premiums which will cover his car to be paid monthly.

## Other costs (all bills and payments include VAT)

| | |
|---|---|
| Rent & rates | £250 per month |
| Postage | £600 per year |
| Telephone | £900 per annum paid quarterly in arrears. The first bill is due in December. |
| Power (heat & light) | £600 per annum paid quarterly in arrears. First account due December. |
| Printing and stationery | £4,000 per annum |

Depreciation on the car and equipment will be 25% of the reducing balance.

Sample *Business Plan*

**This business plan has been prepared for**

**Mike Cunningham t/a**

# SALES LEDGER SERVICES

**FOR THE PERIOD**

**September 2002 to August 2003**

Sample *Business Plan* (continued)

## MISSION STATEMENT

To provide medium and small sized businesses considered too small to have their own credit departments with a full in-house credit control and sales ledger operation. To reduce clients' sales ledger debt and improve customer service, thereby freeing cash tied up needlessly within their sales ledgers.

## BUSINESS OBJECTIVES

1. To commence trading in September 2002. To achieve drawing of £15,000 per annum in the first year of trading and to break even.

2. To have a customer base of 120 by the end of the first years' trading.

3. To achieve drawing and profits of £50,000 in year two.

4. To maintain a continuing professional training policy.

5. To qualify for an 'Investors in People' award, as soon as possible.

6. To provide the best sales ledger, book-keeping and pay-roll service in the area, both on and off clients' premises.

7. To treat staff in a fair and equitable manner.

8. To resolve any customer query in the shortest time possible.

9. To make SLS a happy place to work.

Sample *Business Plan* (continued)

---

### CAPITAL INJECTION

**Owner's Name**                                      **Capital Invested**
Mike Cunningham                                           £20,000

Made up of £15,000 cash, plus Rover 600 car valued at £5,000

### KEY PERSONNEL

Name:                          Mike Cunningham

Position:                      Owner

Qualifications:                Institute of Credit Management I, II, and III

Main responsibilities:         To set up, market, and manage business.
                               Train staff in credit & sales ledger activities

Experience:                    9 years experience in credit and risk
                               management. Credit manager for P&P
                               Commercial Finance Ltd. 3 years Interim
                               Management assignments, installing credit
                               control systems.

---

Sample *Business Plan* (continued)

| | |
|---|---|
| Name: | Karen Swift |
| Position: | Office manager |
| Qualifications: | Institute of Credit Management Parts I and II |
| Main responsibilities: | Support Mike in running business. Setting up client computerised sales ledgers. Attend to customers' problems in person and on the telephone. Assist with recruitment and training |
| Experience: | 3 years credit control experience, of which 2 years was spent at supervisory level at P & P Commercial Finance Ltd. Prior to the previous appointment four years general accountancy experience was gained with HP Finance Ltd. |
| Name: | Linda Cunningham |
| Position: | Part time book-keeper |
| Qualifications: | IAB Diploma in Book-keeping |
| Main responsibilities: | Maintain accounting recorders. Provide book-keeping service for clients. |
| Experience: | No recent experience. |

Sample *Business Plan* (continued)

---

## MARKET REPORT

### MARKET TRENDS

Within the area of initial operation there is a growing tendency to out-source specialised areas of operation. Areas such as book-keeping, payroll, mail room and cleaning.

At the present time, no one in the targeted area is offering a sales ledger service, apart from the major factoring houses. Generally these factors are members of the Factors & Discount Association and usually seek clients with minimum sales of £1 million.

There are no seasonal fluctuations.

In the first year, new clients will increase from 26 to 312. There are no restrictions on expanding the area of operations, once additional resources have been put in place.

Average client profile

Turnover:                       £250,000.

Staff:                          10

Days sales outstanding:         78

Sources of information were from market research and experience gained working for P & P Commercial Finance.

Days sales outstanding means the average time it takes a customer to pay an invoice when the terms of trade are stated as 30 days.

---

Sample *Business Plan* (continued)

## PRICING POLICY

Unit costs are based on the following perimeters, using the average customer profile.

### Sales Ledger services

1 unit = 2 hours sales ledger & collections work in-house. Charged at £17.50 per hour. An average client will require 2 units per month. Therefore unit costs are £35.00 each.

### Book-keeping services

1 unit = an average of 7 hours book-keeping per month. Charged at £12 per hour the average client will need 1 unit per month. Consequently a unit cost £84.00 each.

### Pay-roll services

1 unit = maintaining a monthly wages bill for up to 10 staff. Charged at £12 per hour. Cost per unit is £47.25

## MARKETING PLAN

**Target Market:** Small to medium size firms with less than twenty employees.

**Method of promotion:** Direct mailing, telephone and person contact. It is hoped to address trade association meetings, and talk at Business Link seminars.

**Sales summary (1st Year):** Total fee income £142,000 Gross Promotional expenses £4,000.

Sample *Business Plan* (continued)

# OPERATIONS PLAN

## PREMISES

Sales Ledger services will operate from:

> Suite 9, The Seedbed Centre,
> Nonsuch Road, Anytown,
> Anywhere, ZX12 5YW

**Location:** The premises are located on the edge of a busy market town, close to London, situated adjacent to a major road network offering easy access to nearby towns and industrial estates. A main line station is within walking distance. There is ample car parking facilities for clients and staff.

**Tenure:** The premises will be held primarily on a six month agreement, then monthly thereafter. Rent, which includes rates, and premises insurance amounts to £250 per month payable in advance. A deposit of one month's rent is also required. Sign writing at a cost of £150 is needed. Fitting out a small reception area will cost £600. Telephone and fax lines and machines are already installed.

## MATERIALS

Continuing supply of brochures, letter headings, invoices, statements will be required. The first years' costs are estimated at £4,000.

**Suppliers:** Many printers and stationers are within close proximity, each offering a 24 hour service.

Sample *Business Plan* (continued)

## EMPLOYEES

Initial staffing levels will be:        Full-time        2
                                         Part-time        1

Staffing levels at end of period:       Full-time        6
                                         Part-time        5

**Attendance requirements:**

All staff must be prepared to work at our own offices, and on clients' premises.

## TRAINING

**Linda Cunningham**

Booking-Keeping and business administration

| | |
|---|---|
| Duration: | 4 days |
| Trainer: | Business Link |
| Location: | Small Business Centre |
| Cost: | Free of charge |

**Mike Cunningham and Karen Swift**

Software and system training

| | |
|---|---|
| Duration: | 3 two hour sessions |
| Trainer: | Software & systems provider |
| Location: | SlS's offices |
| Cost: | £300. |

New employees will be trained in software systems at Software Suppliers offices for half day. On job training of SLS's credit control procedures will be on-going.

Sample *Business Plan* (continued)

## EQUIPMENT

6 desks, 8 chairs, 3 filing cabinets will be purchased at auction.

A reception unit is being purpose made. Total cost of these items is £2,000.

2 Desk-top computers and two lap-tops will be leased at a rental of £160 per month, payable by direct debit.

## TRANSPORT

Transportation is fairly important to the business, as it expected some clients will be situated on industrial estates, away from public transport. Getting between clients' premises in the shortest possible time is also important.

Mike's personal car has been transferred to the business and will be used for business and private use. Staff will be required to use their own vehicles for which a mileage allowance of 25p per mile will be paid.

## INSURANCE

A combined contents policy for the office equipment has been taken out. This will also include the lap-top computers which will accompany staff when visiting clients' premises. Professional, Public and Employers liability are also included. The annual premiums of £2,400 are being paid monthly by direct debit.

Employees are to ensure their own vehicle insurance offer suitable cover for using the car to visit clients.

Sample *Business Plan* (continued)

## OBSERVATIONS

### Cash flow forecast

You will note in the forecast illustrated, there will be need for additional short term funding of £7,000 in the first year.

Therefore an interest charge will need to be incorporated within this chart.

### Profit & Loss forecast

The interest element from the loan would also need to be incorporated within this prediction.

A calculation for depreciation was omitted from this forecast due to lack of space, for the business plan example shown. The annual charge for depreciation for Mike's car and office furniture would amount to £1,750 per annum. Computed at 25% of cost.

### Mission statement

Mike's business objectives for the second year will be on track if you continue the forecasts into 2004.

## Sample *Business Plan* (continued)

**SALES LEDGER SERVICES**

**CASH FLOW FORECAST Sept 2002 to August 2003**

| Month | Sept £ | Oct £ | Nov £ | Dec £ | Jan £ | Feb £ | Mar £ | Apr £ | May £ | Jun £ | Jly £ | Aug £ | Total £ |
|---|---|---|---|---|---|---|---|---|---|---|---|---|---|
| **RECEIPTS** | | | | | | | | | | | | | |
| Total sales | 1813 | 3626 | 5439 | 7252 | 9065 | 10878 | 13251 | 14504 | 16317 | 18130 | 19943 | 21756 | 141974 |
| Cash invested | 15000 | | | | | | | | | | | | 15000 |
| **TOTAL RECEIPTS** | 16813 | 3626 | 5439 | 7252 | 9065 | 10878 | 13251 | 14504 | 16317 | 18130 | 19943 | 21756 | 156974 |
| | | | | | | | | | | | | | |
| **PAYMENTS** | | | | | | | | | | | | | |
| Rent/Rates | 250 | 250 | 250 | 250 | 250 | 250 | 250 | 250 | 250 | 250 | 250 | 250 | 3000 |
| Wages | 5000 | 5000 | 7650 | 7650 | 7650 | 10350 | 10350 | 10350 | 10350 | 14000 | 14000 | 15950 | 118300 |
| Printing | 2500 | | | | | 250 | 250 | 250 | 250 | | 250 | 250 | 4000 |
| Telephone | | | 225 | | | 225 | | | 225 | | | 225 | 900 |
| Light/heating | | | 150 | | | 150 | | | 150 | | | 150 | 600 |
| Insurance | 200 | 200 | 200 | 200 | 200 | 200 | 200 | 200 | 200 | 200 | 200 | 200 | 2400 |
| Lease Rentals | 160 | 160 | 160 | 160 | 320 | 320 | 320 | 320 | 480 | 480 | 480 | 480 | 3840 |
| Transport | 60 | 60 | 80 | 70 | 110 | 110 | 120 | 120 | 140 | 140 | 160 | 180 | 1350 |
| Postage | 50 | 50 | 50 | 25 | 75 | 50 | 50 | 50 | 50 | 50 | 50 | 50 | 600 |
| Training | 300 | | | | 300 | | 150 | | | 150 | | | 900 |
| Drawings | 1250 | 1250 | 1250 | 1250 | 1250 | 1250 | 1250 | 1250 | 1250 | 1250 | 1250 | 1250 | 15000 |
| **TOTAL PAYMENTS** | 9770 | 6970 | 10015 | 9605 | 10155 | 13355 | 12940 | 12790 | 12790 | 16520 | 16640 | 18985 | 150535 |
| **NET CASH FLOW** | 7043 | -3344 | -4576 | -2353 | -1090 | -2477 | 311 | 1714 | 3527 | 1610 | 3303 | 2771 | 6439 |
| **CUM. CASH FLOW** | 7043 | 3699 | -877 | -3230 | -4320 | -6797 | -6486 | -4772 | -1245 | 365 | 3668 | 6439 | |

Sample *Business Plan* (continued)

## SALES LEDGER SERVICES

### PROFIT & LOSS FORECAST Sept 2002 to August 2003

| Month | Sept £ | Oct £ | Nov £ | Dec £ | Jan £ | Feb £ | Mar £ | Apr £ | May £ | Jun £ | Jly £ | Aug £ | Total £ |
|---|---|---|---|---|---|---|---|---|---|---|---|---|---|
| **INCOME** | | | | | | | | | | | | | |
| Total sales | 1813 | 3626 | 5439 | 7252 | 9065 | 10878 | 13251 | 14504 | 16317 | 18130 | 19943 | 21756 | 141974 |
| **EXPENDITURE (Variable costs)** | | | | | | | | | | | | | |
| Salaries | 3000 | 3000 | 5650 | 5650 | 5650 | 8350 | 8350 | 8350 | 8350 | 12000 | 12000 | 13950 | 94300 |
| Gross profit | −1187 | 626 | −211 | 1602 | 3415 | 2528 | 4901 | 6154 | 7967 | 6130 | 7943 | 7806 | 47674 |
| **Fixed costs** | | | | | | | | | | | | | |
| Rent/Rates | 250 | 250 | 250 | 250 | 250 | 250 | 250 | 250 | 250 | 250 | 250 | 250 | 3000 |
| Wages | 2000 | 2000 | 2000 | 2000 | 2000 | 2000 | 2000 | 2000 | 2000 | 2000 | 2000 | 2000 | 24000 |
| Printing | 370 | 330 | 330 | 330 | 330 | 330 | 330 | 330 | 330 | 330 | 330 | 330 | 4000 |
| Telephone | 75 | 75 | 75 | 75 | 75 | 75 | 75 | 75 | 75 | 75 | 75 | 75 | 900 |
| Light/heating | 50 | 50 | 50 | 50 | 50 | 50 | 50 | 50 | 50 | 50 | 50 | 50 | 600 |
| Insurance | 200 | 200 | 200 | 200 | 200 | 200 | 200 | 200 | 200 | 200 | 200 | 200 | 2400 |
| Lease Rentals | 160 | 160 | 160 | 160 | 320 | 320 | 320 | 320 | 480 | 480 | 480 | 480 | 3840 |
| Transport | 60 | 60 | 80 | 70 | 110 | 110 | 120 | 120 | 140 | 140 | 160 | 180 | 1350 |
| Postage | 50 | 50 | 50 | 50 | 50 | 50 | 50 | 50 | 50 | 50 | 50 | 50 | 600 |
| Training | 75 | 75 | 75 | 75 | 75 | 75 | 75 | 75 | 75 | 75 | 75 | 75 | 900 |
| Drawings | 1250 | 1250 | 1250 | 1250 | 1250 | 1250 | 1250 | 1250 | 1250 | 1250 | 1250 | 1250 | 15000 |
| **TOTAL FIXED COSTS** | 4540 | 4500 | 4520 | 4510 | 4710 | 4710 | 4720 | 4720 | 4900 | 4900 | 4920 | 4940 | 56590 |
| Total costs | 7540 | 7500 | 10170 | 10160 | 10360 | 13060 | 13070 | 13070 | 13250 | 16900 | 16920 | 18890 | 150890 |
| Net profit/loss | −5727 | −3874 | −4731 | −2908 | −1295 | −2182 | 181 | 1434 | 3067 | 1230 | 3023 | 2866 | −3189 |

Sample *Business Plan* (continued)

## SALES LEDGER SERVICES
### MARKETING FORECAST Sept 2002 to August 2003

| Product/Service | Unit price |
|---|---|
| Sales Ledger Service | £35.00 |
| Book-keeping Service | £84.00 |
| Pay-roll Service | £47.25 |

| Month | | Sept | Oct | Nov | Dec | Jan | Feb | Mar | Apr | May | Jun | Jly | Aug | Total |
|---|---|---|---|---|---|---|---|---|---|---|---|---|---|---|
| **PRODUCT/SERVICE** | | | | | | | | | | | | | | |
| Sales ledger | Units | 32 | 64 | 96 | 128 | 160 | 192 | 240 | 256 | 288 | 320 | 352 | 384 | 2512 |
| | £ | 1120 | 2240 | 3360 | 4480 | 5600 | 6720 | 8400 | 8960 | 10080 | 11200 | 12320 | 13440 | 87920 |
| | Cumulative | 1120 | 3360 | 6720 | 11200 | 16800 | 23520 | 31920 | 40880 | 50960 | 62160 | 74480 | 89920 | |
| Book-keeping | Units | 6 | 12 | 18 | 24 | 30 | 36 | 42 | 48 | 54 | 60 | 66 | 72 | 468 |
| | £ | 504 | 1008 | 1512 | 2016 | 2520 | 3024 | 3528 | 4032 | 4536 | 5040 | 5544 | 6048 | 39312 |
| | Cumulative | 504 | 1512 | 3024 | 5040 | 7560 | 10584 | 14112 | 18144 | 22680 | 27720 | 33264 | 39312 | |
| Pay-roll | Units | 4 | 8 | 12 | 16 | 20 | 24 | 28 | 32 | 36 | 40 | 44 | 48 | 312 |
| | £ | 189 | 378 | 567 | 756 | 945 | 1134 | 1323 | 1512 | 1701 | 1890 | 2079 | 2268 | 14742 |
| | Cumulative | 189 | 567 | 1134 | 1890 | 2835 | 3969 | 5292 | 6804 | 8505 | 10395 | 12474 | 14742 | |
| **Total monthly sales** | £ | 1813 | 3626 | 5439 | 7252 | 9065 | 10878 | 13251 | 14504 | 16317 | 18130 | 19943 | 21756 | 141974 |
| **Total cumulative sales** | £ | 1813 | 5439 | 10870 | 18130 | 27195 | 38073 | 51324 | 65828 | 82145 | 100275 | 120218 | 141974 | |
| **PROMOTIONAL EXPENSES** | | | | | | | | | | | | | | |
| Sales Ledger | | 400 | 400 | 400 | | 300 | 300 | 300 | 300 | 200 | 200 | 300 | 300 | 3400 |
| Book-keeping | | 50 | 25 | 25 | | 25 | 25 | 25 | 25 | 25 | 25 | 25 | 25 | 300 |
| Pay-roll | | 50 | 25 | 25 | | 25 | 25 | 25 | 25 | 25 | 25 | 25 | 25 | 300 |
| **Total monthly promotion** | £ | 500 | 450 | 450 | | 350 | 350 | 350 | 350 | 250 | 250 | 350 | 350 | 4000 |
| **Total cumulative prom.** | £ | 500 | 950 | 1400 | | 1750 | 2100 | 2450 | 2800 | 3050 | 3300 | 3650 | 4000 | |

# Index

## More books available from Law Pack...

### Legal Advice Handbook

Where do you go for legal advice? As the sources of both free and paid-for legal advice become more diverse and specific areas of law demand greater specialisation from the advice givers, the need for a consumer guide to this expanding, unmapped network has never been greater. Solicitor Tessa Shepperson has gathered together extensive research data and produced an invaluable handbook.

| Code B427 | ISBN 1 902646 71 1 | PB |
|---|---|---|
| A5 | 130pp | £7.99 | October 2001 |

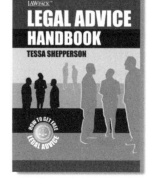

### How to Complain Effectively

Faulty goods, shoddy service, poor advice... these are things most of us, at some time, feel we have good reason to complain about. In this practical guide, Steve Wiseman draws on his extensive experience as a Citizens Advice Bureau manager and tells you how to ensure your complaint has maximum impact, whether it be against your local shop or a government department.

| Code B430 | ISBN 1 902646 80 0 | PB |
|---|---|---|
| A5 | 160pp | £7.99 | May 2001 |

### Tax Answers at a Glance

With the emphasis on self-assessment, we all need to have a hold of the array of taxes now levied by government. Compiled by UK award-winning tax experts, HM Williams Chartered Accountants, and presented in question-and-answer format, this handy guide provides a useful summary of income tax, VAT, capital gains, inheritance, pensions, self-employment, partnerships, land and property, trusts and estates, corporation tax, stamp duty and more.

| Code B425 | ISBN 1 902646 84 3 | PB |
|---|---|---|
| A5 | 192pp | £7.99 | 2nd edition |

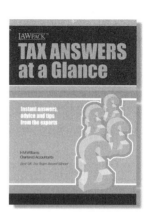

To order, visit www.lawpack.co.uk or call 020 7394 4040

# More MADE EASY books available from Law Pack...

## Employment Law

Written by an employment law solicitor, *Employment Law Made Easy* is a bestelling, comprehensive source of information that will provide reader-friendly answers to practically all your employment law questions. Now in its third edition. Essential knowledge for all employers and employees!

| Code B502 | ISBN 1 904053 08 4 | PB |
|---|---|---|
| 250 x 199mm | 176pp | £9.99 | June 02 |

## Effective PR Made Easy

Raise your profile with some effective PR! Nearly all businesses and organisations benefit from generating public relations activity, be it with customers or other target audiences. The author, Ian Proud, is a seasoned PR professional who tells you from the inside how to get the most out of a PR agency and also how to go about creating effective PR yourself.

| Code B518 | ISBN 1 902646 96 7 | PB |
|---|---|---|
| 250 x 199mm | 120pp | £9.99 | July 02 |

## Limited Company Formation

Incorporation as a limited liability company is the preferred structure for thousands of successful businesses. *Limited Company Formation Made Easy* Guide explains why, and shows you how to set up your own limited liability company easily and inexpensively. It provides detailed but easy to follow instructions, background information, completed examples of Companies House forms and drafts of other necessary documents.

| Code B503 | ISBN 1 902646 43 6 | PB |
|---|---|---|
| 250 x 199mm | 112pp | £9.99 | Oct 99 |

To order, visit www.lawpack.co.uk or call 020 7394 4040

# More MADE EASY books available from Law Pack...

## Company MInutes & Resolutions

*Company Minutes & Resolutions Made Easy* is what every busy company secretary or record-keeper needs. Maintaining good, up-to-date records is not only sensible business practice, but also a legal requirement of Companies House. This *Made Easy* Guide makes the whole process straightforward. It provides an invaluable source of essential documents that no company should be without.

| Code B501 | ISBN 1 902646 41 X | PB |
|---|---|---|
| 250 x 199mm | 190pp £9.99 | Oct 99 |

## Profitable Mail-Order

Mail-order business is big business, and it's growing year by year. Setting up and running your own mail-order business can be fun as well as profitable. This *Made Easy* Guide shows you how to do it, explaining the vital importance of product profile, building valuable mailing lists, effective advertising and a whole lot more. It divulges the mail-order secrets that ensure success!

| Code B510 | ISBN 1 902646 46 0 | PB |
|---|---|---|
| 250 x 199mm | 206pp £9.99 | Oct 99 |

## Debt Collection

Chasing debts is a pain which all businesses can do without. Unfortunately, unpaid bills are an all-too frequent problem for business owners and managers. *Debt Collection Made Easy,* by Roy Hedges, helps you solve it. It provides expert advice and tips on resolving disputes, reducing the risks of bad debt, getting money out of reluctant payers, letter cycles, credit insurance, export credit, and much more.

| Code B512 | ISBN 1 902646 42 8 | PB |
|---|---|---|
| 250 x 199mm | 134pp £9.99 | Oct 99 |

To order, visit www.lawpack.co.uk or call 020 7394 4040